Making Your
CASE FOR
Christ

*An Action Plan for Sharing
What You Believe and Why*

LEE STROBEL *and*
MARK MITTELBERG

ZONDERVAN®

ZONDERVAN

Making Your Case for Christ Study Guide
Copyright © 2018 by Lee Strobel and Mark Mittelberg

This title is also available as a Zondervan ebook.

Requests for information should be addressed to:
Zondervan, *3900 Sparks Dr. SE, Grand Rapids, Michigan 49546*

ISBN 978-0-310-09513-2

Cover image: Shutterstock®
Interior design: Rob Williams

First Printing April 2018 / Printed in the United States of America

Contents

INTRODUCTION

As followers of Christ, we know, at least at some level, that we're on this planet for higher purposes than to simply live out our days and then go to heaven someday. No, we're here for a much greater reason than that.

Jesus explained his *own* purpose for coming to earth. He told us that he, the Son of Man, came "to seek and to save the lost" (Luke 19:10). He was on a mission to reach as many people as possible with his salvation and leadership, which he offered freely to every person.

But Jesus didn't stop there. Before he returned to the Father, he said to his disciples—and, by extension, to *us*—"as the Father has sent me, I am sending you" (John 20:21).

So we, too, are now on Jesus' redemptive mission. Like our leader, we are here "to seek and to save" everyone around us who will listen to the good news of the gospel. "He has committed to us the message of reconciliation," Paul added. "We are therefore Christ's ambassadors, as though God were making his appeal through us" (2 Corinthians 5:19–20).

The question is, what might that appeal look like in our increasingly secular and spiritually resistant society? Our central message does not change, of course, but as Paul put it, "I have become all things to all people so that by all possible means I might save some. I do this for the sake of the gospel, that I may share in its blessings" (1 Corinthians 9:22–23).

In other words, Paul was telling us that we—like him—need to adjust our approach in order to optimally connect our unchanging message to the people in our culture, which has moved further and further away from God.

Part of the answer to the question of what our appeal should look like was articulated by J. Warner Wallace, an atheist-turned-Christian who wrote, "In this day and age, evangelism is spelled: A-P-O-L-O-G-E-T-I-C-S."[1] Along with presenting the straightforward gospel, we need to give our friends reasons for *why* our message makes sense and can be confidently embraced as truth. They're often interested in our message and attracted to our Savior, but they want to make certain that what they're considering putting their trust in is truly trustworthy.

That's where Christian apologetics comes in—it helps us explain the logic and evidence that back up our biblical beliefs, and it helps remove the intellectual barriers that keep people from putting their faith in Christ. This is what we've written about in our books over the years, and now we're presenting it in this unique six-session course, *Making Your Case for Christ*. We've pulled together some of the key elements of relational evangelism as well as applied apologetics to help you clearly articulate what you believe, why it makes sense, and how your friends can find and follow Christ like you have.

Our prayer is that this material, along with your times of discussion in your group and your engagement with it between the sessions, will serve to strengthen your own faith while making you confident in your ability to spread that faith to others.

Lee Strobel and Mark Mittelberg

Note

1. J. Warner Wallace, "In This Day and Age, Evangelism Is Spelled: A-P-O-L-O-G-E-T-I-C-S," http://coldcase christianity.com/2015/in-this-day-and-age-evangelism-is-spelled-a-p-o-l-o-g-e-t-i-c-s/.

HOW TO
USE THIS GUIDE

The goal of the *Making Your Case for Christ* training course is to help you understand and articulate the evidence for the biblical record of Christ as well as the facts pointing to the reality of Jesus' life, death, and resurrection. This course will also help you explain the central message of the gospel to your friends and family members who need salvation, articulate the story of how you came to know Jesus as your Savior, and provide you with practical steps for encouraging—even "nudging"—your loved ones to make their own decision to follow Christ.

This course is designed to be experienced in a small-group setting, such as a home Bible study or a Sunday School class, as there is a unique dynamic when you learn in the context of relationships. Ultimately, the idea is not just to gain knowledge but also to experience life transformation, to grow in friendships, and to apply what you learn in your day-to-day life. After all, what better way to discover how to make your own case for Christ than to be with a group of people who are going through the process with you and learning the same things?

Each participant should have his or her own copy of this study guide, because you will gain much more from this journey if you are able to write notes in it during the sessions and then to use it to reflect more deeply on the topics covered during the week. It is also helpful (though not essential) to obtain a copy of *The Case for Christ* book. The videos and material in this study guide are based on information in that book, which develops more fully many of the ideas discussed here. You and your group may also wish to watch *The Case for Christ* movie in its entirety, as each session in this course contains clips from this film to help illustrate the points Lee Strobel and Mark Mittelberg cover in the teaching videos.

The *Making Your Case for Christ* training course is divided into six sessions—one for each week of the curriculum. Every session contains a *Getting Started* section to introduce the main topic, some *Opening Discussion* questions, *Video Teaching* notes, *Group Interaction* questions, a *Group Reflection*, *Conclusion*, and a *Closing Challenge* and prayer.

As a group, you should plan to discuss the opening questions, watch the video, and then use the video notes and questions to engage with the topic. There is complete freedom to decide how best to use these elements to meet the needs of your members. Again, the goal is developing relationships and becoming better equipped to share the evidence for Christ with your friends and family members who need to know God—not just "covering the material." You are encouraged to explore each topic as a group and discover what God is saying to you.

These times together as a group can be rewarding, refreshing, and often life-changing. Things might feel a little forced or awkward at first, but don't worry. The members of your group will soon become trusted companions. There is something about learning and praying together that is healthy and invigorating for the human soul.

It is important to maintain a positive and safe environment in the group. The group members should have an opportunity to share what they are learning to the extent they feel comfortable. Don't feel obligated to participate, but don't keep silent if you have something that contributes to the discussion. People need to hear what you have to say!

On the other hand, no one should dominate the conversation or impose his or her opinions on others. The group discussion time is a conversation, not a monologue or a debate, and differing views are welcome. People are encouraged to share their emotions, challenges, and struggles honestly, without fear of rejection or ridicule. And, of course, it is especially important to maintain confidentiality regarding what is said.

At the end of each group session, there are three optional *Between-Sessions* activities that you are invited to complete during the week. In the first section, *Study God's Word*, you will examine three key passages of Scripture that pertain to the topic you covered during the group time. The next section, *Put It into Practice*, will help you develop natural ways to act on the challenge you were given at the end of the group time. In the final section, *Reflect on a Key Story*, you will review a short reading from the book *The Unexpected Adventure* by Strobel and Mittelberg and answer some reflection questions on how to apply its principles to your life.

The goal is simply to engage with these topics on a personal level. You won't be required to divulge what you write, but starting in session two, you will be given time at the beginning of the meeting to discuss any key takeaways you gained or questions that arose as you did the activities. Often, sharing in such a manner is the best way to learn and grow, and you might be surprised at how helpful your thoughts are to others. If you have a busy week and can't get to these activities, don't worry. You are always welcome at the group meetings—ready or not!

Ask for and expect the Holy Spirit to speak to you as you go through this course. It's not an accident that you have chosen to participate in this six-week journey. God has great things in store for you, and he will speak to you in ways you might not expect. So take time to pray and meditate on what he is saying. You might want to write down some thoughts for future reference. This is the beginning of a deeper journey with Jesus, and the Holy Spirit will be with you as you seek to *make your case for Christ* to those in your life who need God's touch.

Note: *If you are a group leader, there are additional instructions and resources in the back of this guide to help you lead your members through the study.*

HELPING FRIENDS CONSIDER THE CASE FOR CHRIST

*My only aim is to finish the race and
complete the task the Lord Jesus has given me—
the task of testifying to the good news of God's grace.*

ACTS 20:24

Getting Started

Welcome to session one of *Making Your Case for Christ*. We're glad you decided to join us, and we hope you'll be able to continue with the group throughout the rest of these six sessions. Together, we'll learn about how we can better understand, explain, and defend our beliefs as Christians.

Opening Discussion

It's likely that you grew up going to church, hearing Bible stories, memorizing verses, and singing worship songs. That's a great heritage, and it's certainly something to be thankful for. But it can also lead to assuming that the people around you know what you know, or at least understand what you believe and why it makes sense.

But the reality is that more and more people are growing up today without any sort of solid biblical teaching or understanding. If they believe in God at all it's often a fuzzy, generic belief—not a clear understanding of who Jesus really is, why they should trust in him, and the difference it will make in their lives, both today and for eternity.

These people may not know God, but God still loves them and wants to reach them with his offer of forgiveness through Christ. And whether they be in your school, your workplace, your neighborhood, or even your family, Jesus said to "go and make disciples . . . teaching them to obey everything I have commanded you" (Matthew 28:19–20).

"Go and make disciples . . . teaching them to obey everything I have commanded you." — Matthew 28:19-20

To do this effectively, you're going to have to be clear about *what* you believe and some of the reasons *why* you can be confident it is true. Put another way, you need to be ready to make your own case for Christ. That's what this six-week study is designed to help you do.

As we begin, let's read together a verse that sets the foundation for all of our discussions: *"In your hearts revere Christ as Lord. Always be prepared to give an answer to everyone who asks you to give the reason for the hope that you have. But do this with gentleness and respect"* (1 Peter 3:15). There are four key elements in this verse. Let's talk about each of them briefly.

- The first phrase says we need to "revere Christ as _____." Why do you think Peter mentions this first? Have you ever seen people try to help others spiritually without making sure that they were right with God themselves? What were the results?

- The second element says we need to "always be _____." Can you imagine a sports team going into an important game without doing good preparation ahead of time? (Maybe a team comes to mind?) The good news is that you're here today—doing some of the preparation Peter was talking about.

- The third element is the focus of our preparation—to be ready "to give _____ _____" to anyone who asks you for the reasons behind your faith in Christ. As we'll discuss today, a lot of people are just a few good answers away from taking the gospel seriously. So, you need to be ready to give them those answers.

- The final phrase in the verse says that you should give your answers "with _____ _____ _____" (some translations list this as verse 16). You live in a culture in which these attributes are hard to find, especially in social media and other online interactions. Why do you think it's so important to address spiritually curious people in a gentle and respectful way?

Getting yourself prepared and taking the kind of approach Peter prescribes will go a long way toward helping your friends understand and consider the case for Christ.

▶ Video Teaching

Now watch the video for session one, in which you'll meet the authors of this course, Lee Strobel and Mark Mittelberg, and hear them discuss the topic of this session: "Helping Friends Consider the Case for Christ." As you watch, use the following outline to record any thoughts or concepts that stand out to you.

Opening Vignette

Some people say, "You can't argue a person into the kingdom of God." While that's true—you need more than just information—evidence and apologetics can play a critical part in breaking down the barriers in that person's journey toward Christ.

Truth & love is too hard
Love & truth is too soft

Main Teaching

First Peter 3:15 is the imperative that tells us we need to be prepared to give an answer for the hope we have in Christ—and give it gently and with respect.

John Stott said, "Truth without love is too hard, and love without truth is too soft." Jesus had the perfect balance, and he's calling us to seek the same balance.

We need to look into the evidence for our faith. We need to know *why we believe what we believe.* As we gain that knowledge, it will help grow our confidence to share our faith with others.

In the Bible, we read of at least two examples in which Jesus provided evidence to back up his claim that he was the Son of God:

> John the Baptist testified that Jesus was the Son of God, but doubts crept in when he was thrown in prison. Jesus told his followers to go back to John and tell them about the evidence they had seen with their own eyes.

> The disciple Thomas questioned that Jesus had risen from the dead. Jesus did not shame him, but instead he told Thomas, *Look at the holes in my hands and the scars in my side. Check out the evidence for yourself.*

Paul would sum up his ministry by saying, *We do what we do to persuade people. We want people to know our claims about Jesus are true.*

It is necessary in the kind of culture we live in today, in which people have moved away from a Christian worldview, to be prepared to give an answer for the hope we have in Jesus.

We tend to think people are resistant to hearing the gospel, but the reality is that *we* are the ones who are often more afraid to talk about it! People *want* to talk about spiritual matters.

Movie Clip

In the first scene at the restaurant, see how Alfie brings up spiritual matters after the events surrounding Alison have taken place there.

In the second scene in the car, notice how Alfie asks questions and talks honestly with Leslie about matters of faith.

Video Wrap

It pays to have our antennae up, watching for the opportunities God brings our way to engage people in conversations about Christ.

"Then you will know the truth, and the truth will set you free." — John 8:32

 Group Interaction

We've seen how important good answers and information were in the testimonies of both Lee and Mark. We also heard them emphasize the fact that we'll never be able to give our friends that kind of information unless we first initiate conversations about spiritual matters with them. Alfie did just that in the movie clip we watched during the teaching. Let's discuss what she did and how it worked.

- In the first scene, Alfie explained that she wasn't at that restaurant, and therefore able to help little Alison, due to mere luck. Instead, she credited Jesus for leading her there that night. Did Alfie's way of explaining that feel natural to you? What might you have said differently to bring up spiritual matters in that situation?

- You might think that what Alfie said was a little forced. But what would have happened if she hadn't taken that risk? Or maybe a better question: what would *not* have happened? Have you taken a similar risk—one that might have felt a bit unnatural, but God used it anyway? How did it turn out?

- In the movie, when Alfie and Leslie talked again, Alfie invited Leslie to come to church with her, and Leslie accepted the invitation. Have you ever invited a friend to church or some other Christian gathering as a way to further your spiritual interactions with them? What happened?

- In the second part of the movie clip, you saw Alfie and Leslie talking in the car after they had gone to church together. What kinds of questions did Alfie ask Leslie? Have you ever just come out and asked your spiritually curious friends about their beliefs or religious background? How have they responded?

Group Reflection

Let's summarize some of what Alfie did well in order to help Leslie:

1. Alfie *served* Leslie (and Lee) by intervening to help their daughter.
2. She *mentioned Jesus* as the source of her ability to help Alison.
3. She gradually *formed a friendship* with Leslie.
4. She *invited* Leslie into an environment where Leslie could learn more about matters of faith.
5. She *asked good questions*, drawing Leslie deeper into conversation.

Now let's discuss ways we can apply these lessons from Alfie in our own relationships (if your group is large, break into circles of four to six people). Take a few minutes to discuss the following questions:

• Who could you serve this week in ways that might help them open up to God's love? What could you do to best assist them? Are you willing to reach out and serve in that way soon?

• Who do you think you could have a real friendship with, and what practical steps could you take to initiate that kind of relationship? Often, we sense that a neighbor, classmate, or coworker would enjoy getting together and going deeper, but we've been too busy or preoccupied. Does anyone come to mind? What might you do this week to initiate or deepen a real friendship? Write down any names or ideas that come to mind here.

• Maybe you've already been serving or spending time with someone you'd like to share your faith with, but spiritual topics just don't ever seem to come up. What could you say that would feel natural, but jump-start the conversation? Try to think of several possibilities, and write down any thoughts or plans here.

• Alfie inviting Leslie to attend church with her was an important part of Leslie's spiritual journey (and Leslie's later invitation to Lee played a major part in his journey, too). So, who might you invite this week? And what should you invite them to? A church service? A study group? An inspiring concert or film? Maybe ask them to watch *The Case for Christ* movie with you? Maybe a reading or crafts group with some Christian friends? A sporting event or fitness club? Other ideas?

If you broke into smaller groups for the above interactions—and if you have the time—ask for members to share a few of their responses and plans with the whole group.

 ## Conclusion

This session has been about how we can encourage our friends to consider the case for Christ. But before we can go deep into the reasons to trust in him, we first need to deepen their trust in *us*—including seeing that we're safe to talk to about these important but personal matters. We saw from 1 Peter 3:15 that God wants us to *"revere Christ as Lord,"* to *"be prepared"* so we can *"give an answer"* to our friends who have spiritual questions, but to do so *"with gentleness and respect."* We also learned from the example of Alfie that God can use us when we *serve people, build genuine friendships, initiate spiritual conversations, invite friends to appropriate events,* and *ask good questions.* The decision to make now is this: will *we* do these things?

Closing Challenge

As you may have already seen in the later parts of *The Case for Christ* movie, Alfie's small step of mentioning Jesus in the restaurant started a spiritual chain reaction that ultimately led to Leslie, Lee, Alison, and their newborn son Kyle, all eventually coming to faith in Christ. More than that, countless others have come to faith through Lee's books and talks, Leslie's friendships, and the movie itself. Like Alfie, we also need to be willing to take small steps of obedience to God—and he delights in turning them into results we can't even begin to imagine. So, will you take some small steps—little risks with the people you know—this week?

> *"Our purpose is to reach people with the message of Christ, to see them put their trust in him, and to see their lives and eternities change as well."*

Finishing the Session

For more ideas and examples on how you can start spiritual conversations, see the story-driven book, *The Unexpected Adventure,* also by Strobel and Mittelberg. It consists of six weeks of daily readings that will inspire you to bring up your faith in everyday conversations. Close by praying together and asking God to give every group member wisdom, courage, and opportunities to initiate spiritual conversations in order to tell others about Christ, and why it makes sense to follow him.

PERSONAL STUDY

Reflect on the content you've covered this week in *Making Your Case for Christ* by engaging in any or all of the following *between-sessions* activities. The time you invest will be well spent, so let God use it to draw you closer to him. At your next meeting, there will be time for you to share with your group any key points or insights that stood out to you.

Study God's Word

In the following section, we'll examine three key Bible verses related to helping our friends consider trusting in Christ, followed by three reflection questions under each verse.

The Priority of Sharing Your Faith

In Acts 20:24, Paul said, "I consider my life worth nothing to me; my only aim is to finish the race and complete the task the Lord Jesus has given me—the task of testifying to the good news of God's grace."

Why do you think Paul had such urgency about sharing the message of Christ with others?

Reflect on your own priorities. What are some of the activities that make it difficult for you to find time and opportunities to share Christ with others? How might you rearrange your life to create more availability to reach out to them?

What practical steps might you take this week to elevate your own sense of urgency in sharing Christ with others?

Taking the Initiative in Sharing Your Faith

In Romans 10:14, Paul asks a string of poignant questions: "But how can they call on him to save them unless they believe in him? And how can they believe in him if they have never heard about him? And how can they hear about him unless someone tells them?" (NLT).

According to these leading questions from Paul, whose job is it to seek out others and initiate spiritual conversations? The person who is far from God? Or is it God's job? What is our role?

Thinking over the past few months, how many spiritual conversations have you had with people who came and initiated those conversations with you? How many spiritual interactions happened—or perhaps might have happened—after *you* brought up the topic with them?

What friends or family members do you sense God prompting you to talk to about spiritual matters? Can you think of something you might say to bring up the subject? Or is there an event you could invite them to in order to help get the conversation going?

God's Help in Sharing Your Faith

In Matthew 28:18–20, Jesus challenges us with what is commonly referred to as the Great Commission: "All authority in heaven and on earth has been given to me. Therefore go and make disciples of all nations, baptizing them in the name of the Father and of the Son and of the Holy Spirit, and teaching them to obey everything I have commanded you. And surely I am with you always, to the very end of the age."

In the middle of that passage, Jesus gives his disciples—and, by extension, *us*—a strong challenge. What does he tell you there, as his follower, that he wants you to do?

Jesus has given us an important task. Do you feel up to it? If not, then consider the encouraging news he tells us in the beginning of that passage. How much authority has he been given—and in which domains? Are there any limits to his authority?

So, the one who has *all* authority has issued us a daunting assignment: to go into our world and make disciples. But does he send us out alone? Besides having each other to partner with in this endeavor, who else does he say at the end of the passage will go with us? And for how long will he be there for us? How does *that* news change your feelings about the task ahead?

Put It into Practice

In this session, we talked about ways we could initiate spiritual conversations with our friends. Take a moment right now to think and pray about the person in your life whom you most sense God prompting you to reach out to.

What is his or her name? _____

Where would it be most natural for you to talk with this person?

What kinds of subjects do you normally have conversations about?

Now, write down two to three ideas for ways you could turn those topics into spiritual conversations—whether by bridging from the topic being discussed to one of a biblical nature, or by asking that person some questions about their own faith background, or maybe by inviting them to a Christian event of some kind. Write down your ideas, and then prayerfully ask God to allow you to put at least one of them into practice this week.

 # Reflect on a Key Story

The following is a story Mark Mittelberg tells in the book he wrote with Lee Strobel called *The Unexpected Adventure*. It is from the chapter titled, "Being Your Own Eccentric Self." Read this story, and then reflect on the questions that immediately follow.

Being Your Own Eccentric Self

Mark Mittelberg

"Let me know if you have any questions," said the waiter as he leaned against a pillar in our out-of-the-way section of a popular restaurant.

It was an exciting but stressful time in my life. Heidi and I had recently moved from our small Midwestern hometown to the big city of Chicago so I could attend graduate school. With a background in business, I was feeling overwhelmed as I began to work on my master's degree in philosophy of religion.

It wasn't that I didn't enjoy the new subject matter or appreciate my professors. I found the studies fascinating. But have you ever tried to *read* any of Kant's *Critique of Pure Reason*? Try the opening sentence: "In whatever manner and by whatever means a mode of knowledge may relate to objects, intuition is that through which it is in immediate relation to them, and to which all thought as a means is directed."

I don't know about you, but I was pretty sure I could have survived in life without ever having read that information. I was often tempted to ask the question that students frequently ponder: "Are we ever going to really *use* any of this stuff, or is this just a way to see who's fully committed to getting a degree?"

My mind was full of those kinds of thoughts that evening as Heidi and I, along with some new friends from school, sat down at this well-known Italian eatery. The aroma of freshly baked Chicago-style stuffed pizzas wafted through the air. The waiter who seated us was friendly and outgoing. It was after he had gotten us our drinks that he leaned against the pillar and posed his offer to answer any questions we might have.

The restaurant was starting to fill up, causing the rest of the waiters and waitresses to scurry around in order to handle the surge of people. So I was surprised that he was so casually lingering by our table—until I realized that we were in an area that was out of the sight of his boss. The waiter was using us as an occasion for a break. I think he was hoping we would have questions about, say, how they tossed their pizza dough or what ingredients went into their sauce. Just so he wouldn't have to move his feet for a few minutes.

What struck me was how open-ended his offer had been. He had simply invited us to tell him if we had any questions—but he hadn't specified that they needed to be related to the menu. An idea hit me, and it came with enough force that I wondered if the Holy Spirit might be prompting it: *I've got all kinds of questions. Maybe I'll put what I've been reading from Kant to good use, raise an unusual topic, and see what happens,* I thought. *Perhaps God could use it to get us talking about things that matter more than good pizza.*

As a question began forming in my mind, doubts started to creep in as well. *He's going to think I'm really weird—and so will my wife and our new friends.* But I also thought it was strange that he was just standing there, as if he was waiting for something to happen.

"Yes," I piped up cheerfully. "I have an important question."

"Great!" he replied. "What is it?"

"I've been reading Immanuel Kant, and I was wondering," I said with feigned curiosity, "do you think that the categories of the mind apply to the noumenal world in the same way they apply to the phenomenal world?" (I was fairly sure I knew what I was talking about, but at any rate I felt safe that he wouldn't know one way or the other.)

He looked at me, surprised. Then he smiled and shot back with a spirited tone, "I'm not sure, but I once heard about a scientist who looked through his telescope and thought he saw God. Pretty strange, huh?"

"That's not at all strange," I said, amazed at his response. "I don't know if this was the guy you heard about, but I recently read a really interesting book by a well-known scientist named Robert Jastrow, called *God and the Astronomers*. It was his observation of the incredible order and intricacy of the universe that led him to finally conclude that there must be a God. His book shook up a lot of people in the scientific community."

"Wow, that's interesting," he said. "I really don't think about God too much. What did you say the name of that book was?"

Suddenly, we were off to the races in a fascinating spiritual conversation. Before I knew it, I was explaining some of the scientific evidence that supports our Christian beliefs, and a couple of us described the difference Christ had made in our lives.

We eventually got around to figuring out what kind of pizza to order, but I don't remember much about the food that night. What stands out in my mind was the surprising discussion we had and how it all resulted from what felt at the time like a crazy impulse to throw out an unusual remark.

Our interactions didn't end with that encounter. I asked him if he would be interested in reading Jastrow's book, and he said he would. So a few days later I brought him my copy, along with a couple of other smaller books I thought would provide good answers to some of his spiritual questions.

He seemed sincerely grateful for the information. And although I never had the chance to interact with him after that, I'm glad I took a little risk that night by tossing out a playful and unexpected question. As a result, look what happened: on an evening when we were anticipating only a quiet informal dinner, the four of us got the chance to tell someone about Jesus, and I was later able to put some potentially life-changing materials into his hands.

Who knows how God will ultimately use this impromptu interaction in his life? It makes our hot and spicy pizza—as good as it was—seem bland by comparison.

Have you ever sensed that God was prompting you to say something that could lead into a spiritual conversation but might be viewed as a bit unusual? Did you take the risk? Where did it lead?

It's easy to get bottled up in these kinds of situations, held back by fear about how you'll look or sound if you say what came into your mind. But if God is leading, what's the real downside of taking this small risk? How might God use it?

Notice in the story how Mark not only took a risk to get a spiritual conversation started but also followed through—not only by having a real discussion with the waiter, but also by bringing him a copy of the book he had mentioned. How do you think this maximized the impact that he had with the waiter?

In Colossians 4:5, Paul tells each of us to "Be wise in the way you act toward outsiders; make the most of every opportunity." What situation are you in that has an open door for you to take things further spiritually? What's the next step? Will you write it down—and then act on it this week?

DESCRIBING YOUR OWN JOURNEY WITH CHRIST

We proclaim to you what we have seen and heard, so that you also may have fellowship with us. And our fellowship is with the Father and with his Son, Jesus Christ.

1 JOHN 1:3

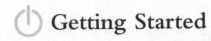 Getting Started

Welcome back! In this session, we're going to get really practical concerning how we can share with others what Christ has done in our own lives. In fact, one of the most persuasive arguments we can make for the case for Christ is a personal one—showing how he has changed *us*! But before we dive into that topic, let's pick up where we ended last time—by talking about any efforts we might have made this past week to start, or continue, a spiritual conversation with someone. Do you have any stories about doors God has opened for you to talk to someone about him? Also, if anyone has any thoughts or questions based on your *between-sessions* personal study times, this is a good time to raise those as well.

Opening Discussion

"It's hard to argue with a life so well lived!" That's what President Bill Clinton said in 1994 after Mother Teresa gave a rousing talk at the National Prayer Breakfast in Washington, D.C. Clinton said this in spite of—or perhaps *because of*—the fact that she had spoken strongly on behalf of the unborn, thus challenging his pro-choice position. His response to her was poignant, and one that applies in a much broader context. When our life reflects the truth of the gospel, the message of that gospel becomes much more compelling.

> *"You are the light of the world . . . let your light shine before others, that they may see your good deeds and glorify your Father in heaven." — Matthew 5:14, 16*

"A person can argue all day with you about certain facts," Greg Laurie said in his book *Tell Someone*. "But they cannot argue with your personal story of how you came to faith."[1]

- Have you ever been in a situation where you were trying to share the truth of Christianity with someone who was resistant, but then saw that person open up when he or she heard some of the details about your own spiritual journey?

- Or have you ever told someone else's story to help illustrate the difference Christ can make in a person's life? Was that approach helpful?

- Maybe you were the resistant person who opened up after hearing about God's activity in the life of someone else. Do you have a story like that?

In the updated and expanded version of *The Case for Christ*, there is a chapter in which Lee relates a variety of amazing stories about people who have come to faith after reading his story and hearing the evidence that convinced him. And, more recently, many others have come to Christ through seeing Lee's story portrayed in *The Case for Christ* movie.

▶ Video Teaching

Now watch the video for session two, in which Lee and Mark discuss the topic of this session: "Describing Your Own Journey with Christ." As you watch, use the following outline to record any thoughts or concepts that stand out to you.

Opening Vignette

There is power in a changed life and a well-articulated testimony. The stories of what God has done in our lives is compelling and persuasive—and impossible to refute.

Main Teaching

It has been said that while people can argue with our facts about Christ, they can't argue with our experience of what God has done personally in our lives. God will use our personal stories to encourage and help others.

An effective way to think through and describe our spiritual story is by using three categories, each beginning with the letter D:

D _Iscover_ : *What did I learn that shaped my spiritual journey?*

D _ecision_ : *What did I do about what I discovered?*

D _ifference_ : *What impact has that decision made in my life?*

Discovering the evidence for Christ often leads to a person making a *Decision* to receive Christ—which then makes a profound *Difference* in his or her life (see 2 Corinthians 5:17).

This framework allows even those who came to faith in their childhood to express their stories in a relevant and practical manner.

Movie Clip

In the movie clip, watch how Leslie approaches her atheist husband, Lee, and tells him that she has come to faith in Christ.

Video Wrap

Notice how the three *D*s play out in Leslie's story:

Discovery—

Decision—

Difference—

The difference God makes in our lives is winsome and attractive to others—and it can help pull them toward making their own decision of faith.

 Group Interaction

It's great to hear how God uses other people's testimonies, but the title of this session is "Describing Your *Own* Journey with Christ"—so that's what we want to work on now. In order to do that, let's reflect on how each of us came to faith by focusing on the three areas Mark talked about in the video: *Discovery, Decision,* and *Difference.* Here they are . . . let's take a few minutes to write down some thoughts under each of the following.

- **Discovery.** What did you learn in your life that helped you reach the conclusion that you needed Christ and the salvation he offers? Was it when you were a child? Was it a process (it usually is)—or maybe a series of discoveries? Who or what were the main influences on your thinking? Were you immediately open, or was it a more gradual journey? Make some notes below about your own spiritual discovery process:

- **Decision.** Describe what you finally decided to do based on what you had discovered, as mentioned above. This might have been a series of decisions—for example, to search more deeply, to attend a discussion group or church service, or to talk to someone about your spiritual questions. However, be sure to include the ultimate decision you made to ask God for his forgiveness and leadership in your life, based on Jesus' payment on the cross for your sins. Also, try to explain what you did in terms that your friend could imitate by being specific about what you understood, decided, prayed, etc. Make some notes below about the details of your decision:

- **Difference.** One of the most important aspects of our testimony (especially to a friend who is trying to decide whether it's worth it to follow Christ) is the difference it has made in your life. What have been the benefits? We need to be careful here not to describe the Christian life in flowery or overstated terms or to promise something the Bible does not promise: a life of unending success and happiness. But, yes, following Jesus is *better*. Jesus said he would give rest to the weary, and in John 10:10 he explained that he came so we "may have life, and have it to the full." He also said "whoever loses their life for my sake will find it" (Matthew 10:39). So, try to paint a positive but realistic picture, based on your own experience, of why it's better to follow Christ. Write down some thoughts about how you might do this:

Now that we've taken time to consider our stories and write down some notes detailing our own *Discovery, Decision,* and *Difference* process, briefly review them and circle or highlight a few key points. You will then be given the chance to tell your story to one other person in the group. (Take several minutes first to review.)

Pair up with someone else—preferably somebody *other than* your spouse or close friend. Then take about three or four minutes each to tell the other person the story about your journey to Christ. (Have someone let the group know when four minutes is up so the other person can also share his or her story. That person can announce again when another four minutes is up.)

"At some point you begin to learn and discover some spiritual truth. The fact that you need a savior. That you're a sinner. That God is real. That Jesus really is who he claimed to be."

Note: If there are those in the group who have not yet made the decision to follow Christ, they can still talk about their spiritual journey thus far, as well as where they think it might lead next. Better yet, they can pray to receive salvation right now, with the encouragement and support of their loving Christian friends cheering them on! Or, if they would prefer, they can just listen in as two other group members share their stories.

Group Reflection

Once you and the other person have finished sharing your stories about Christ, return to the main group and discuss the following questions about the experience.

- How did it go? Did you enjoy talking about God's activity in your life? (Most people find it really encouraging to recount what God has done for them.)

- Is there something you would do differently next time you tell your story? (Remember what you would change, so you can do that this week when you share it with someone else!)

- Did anyone make a decision today to take the next steps in his or her own spiritual journey?

- Would anyone like to briefly share their story with the rest of the group?

 ## Conclusion

In reality, we go through a series of *Discoveries* and *Decisions*, and experience the *Differences*, throughout our spiritual journeys. Also, as followers of Christ, we continue to discover more about God and his will for us, and as we take steps to obey and follow him, we see more and more of those positive differences in our lives. So, we actually have a number of stories within our broader testimony, and we can draw from those as needed to best relate our experience to the person we're trying to reach. But, all of that said, the ultimate *Discovery, Decision, Difference* we need to explain is the one related to our having found salvation through Christ.

Closing Challenge

If you're a follower of Christ, you have an important story to tell. Don't underestimate how God might use it. Also, don't be intimidated when you share it with friends and they say, "That's great—for you. I don't think it's something for my life, but I'm glad you found what you found." You can gently but confidently reply that it's based on what Jesus did for *all* of us, so if it's true for you then it's true for them too. Urge them to look into it further, keeping their mind open to what God might want to do in their life.

> *"If you're a follower of Christ, you have an important story to tell. Don't underestimate how God might use it."*

Testimonies can be powerful, even when they're not your own. Mark often tells Lee's story of coming from atheism to faith, especially when he's talking to an atheist (and he often gives away copies of *The Case for Christ* book and movie as well). But when he talks to Muslims, he often recounts the story of his late friend, Nabeel Qureshi, and gives away Nabeel's book *Seeking Allah, Finding Jesus*. The point is we can utilize stories of lives changed by Christ—including our own and those of others—in our efforts to share our faith with friends.

This week, try to tell at least one person your story of spiritual *Discovery*, *Decision*, and the *Difference* it has made in your life. Then let's hear some reports about how it went at the beginning of the next session!

 ## Finishing the Session

As we close, let's pray together in pairs for the primary person in our life with whom we would like to make our case for Christ. It's probably the person you've been thinking about as we've prepared and practiced telling our stories during this session. Just tell one other person who you're thinking about, what your relationship is to that individual, and then let the other person tell you the same things about his or her person. Then pray together, asking God to open these friends up to the truth of the Christian faith and to soon bring them to Christ himself. (After a few moments, the leader can close the group in prayer.)

BETWEEN-SESSIONS
PERSONAL STUDY

Reflect on the content we've covered this week in *Making Your Case for Christ* by engaging in any or all of the following *between-sessions* activities. The time you invest will be well spent, so let God use it to draw you closer to him. At your next meeting there will be time for you to share with your group any key points or insights that stood out to you.

📖 Study God's Word

In the following section, we'll examine three key Bible verses related to how we can describe our own journey with Christ, followed by three reflection questions under each verse.

Paul Makes a *Discovery*

In Acts 26:9–18, Paul described what his life was like before meeting Jesus. He was a persecutor of the church who thought he was serving God by trying to stamp out this fledgling movement of heretical Christ-followers. Read that passage, and then reflect on these questions.

How would you describe the monumental discovery Paul made that fateful day on his journey to Damascus?

Jesus said in Matthew 7:7–8 that if we seek, we will find. But sometimes, as in this story about Paul, we discover things we weren't seeking at all. In your own story, did you discover things you weren't expecting or looking for? Explain.

What lessons can you draw from Paul's story about the need to be humble and open to God's leadership in your life—including in areas you weren't really wanting to change?

Paul Makes a *Decision*

In Acts 26:19, Paul went on to explain, "So then, King Agrippa, I was not disobedient to the vision from heaven." That's quite an understatement about the life-changing decision Paul made to stop persecuting the church and, instead, become a leader in spreading the Christian message throughout the world! For more details about that decision, read Paul's story in Acts 9:1–19, and then reflect on these questions.

Paul's story reminds us that God knows how to get our attention when he wants to! Did God need to do something in your life to get your attention? In what way?

Are there people in your life who seem to need a wake-up from God so they'll begin to take him and his offer of salvation seriously? How can you pray for them to that end?

It is startling to see how quickly Paul turned from *chief prosecutor* to *lead missionary* of the church. Acts 9:18 casually mentions that after Ananias prayed for him, "He got up and was baptized." That's the kind of step many people consider for months or even years before taking action. Is there a next step of obedience God is calling you to take that Paul's example might inspire you to act upon? What is it?

Paul's Life Exhibits a *Difference*

Going back to Acts 26, we see in verses 20–23 how starkly different Paul's life soon became. Read those verses and consider the following questions.

It's obvious from this passage that Paul took his decision to follow Jesus very seriously. That's undoubtedly why he grew so quickly in his faith and was used by God so powerfully. What Christians in your life exhibit this kind of radical commitment?

Our goal should not be to do exactly what Paul did, or to try to become a clone of the Christians we admire. Rather, we need to find our own God-given gifts and calling. That said, are there steps of obedience to God that these people inspire you to take?

As you prayerfully consider your answer to the last question, what kinds of actions will you take as a result? Is there a Christian confidant you should share this plan with in order to gain his or her encouragement and accountability? Be encouraged by the fact that your courageous obedience to Christ will help those around you be inspired by the difference God can make in a life—including their own.

 ## Put It into Practice

In light of the example of Paul that you just studied, go back now to the pages in session two where you wrote out some of the elements of your story using the three *Ds*: *Discover, Decide,* and *Difference.* Upon further reflection, what would you add or change to what you wrote? Do you need to be a bit more vulnerable about what you've learned or about some of the hard choices you've made to follow Christ? Were there setbacks you should include—along with examples of how God helped you through them?

Spend some time considering and then rounding out what you can say related to God's activity in your life. Once you feel you have a good handle on how you want to convey your story, call a friend and ask him or her if you could have a few minutes to describe it to them. (If it helps, tell your friend it's an assignment for a class you're taking!) This can be a fellow Christian, as telling your story over and over is the best way to refine and become comfortable talking about it. But make it your goal to also share your testimony soon with someone outside the church who might be spiritually impacted when he or she hears about God's activity in your life.

 ## Reflect on a Key Story

The following is an inspiring story Lee Strobel tells in *The Unexpected Adventure*. Take a couple minutes to read it, and then reflect on the four questions that follow it.

The Influence of a Story

Lee Strobel

He was a hard-drinking, glue-sniffing, drug-abusing, hate-filled urban terrorist who had been in and out of the court system ever since he threw a hammer at someone's head when he was eight years old. He rose to second-in-command of the Belaires, a vicious street gang that ruled parts of Chicago. And ironically, he became a significant influence in my journey toward Christ.

How did he do it? As you'll see, Ron Bronski did something that anyone can emulate and that God can powerfully use as we reach out to others.

After various scrapes with the law, Ron got into big-time trouble when he was twenty-one. A member of a rival street gang brutally assaulted one of Ron's friends, and Ron vowed revenge. Soon he tracked down the assailant's brother, whose name was Gary. Ron thrust a gun in Gary's chest—and pulled the trigger.

Click.

The gun misfired. Ron pointed the gun in the air and pulled the trigger again; this time it went off. Gary fled down the sidewalk with Ron in pursuit, shooting as he ran. Finally one of the bullets found its mark, tearing into Gary's back and lodging next to his liver. He fell face forward on the pavement.

Ron flipped him over. "Don't shoot me, man!" Gary pleaded. "Don't shoot me again! Don't kill me!"

Without an ounce of compassion or a moment of hesitation, Ron shoved the gun in Gary's face and pulled the trigger once more.

Click. This time the gun was empty.

A siren wailed in the distance. Ron managed to escape the police, but they issued a warrant for his arrest on a charge of attempted murder. With his previous police record, that would mean twenty years in the penitentiary. To avoid prosecution, Ron and his girlfriend fled Chicago and ended up in Portland, Oregon, where Ron got his first legitimate job, working in a metal shop.

By divine coincidence his coworkers were Christians, and through their influence and the work of the Holy Spirit, Ron became a radically committed follower of Jesus.

Over time, Ron's character and values changed. His girlfriend also became a Christian and they got married. Ron became a model employee, an active church participant, and a well-respected member of the community. The Chicago police had stopped looking for him long ago. He was safe to live out the rest of his days in Portland.

Except that his conscience bothered him. Even though he had been reconciled with God, he hadn't been reconciled with society. He was living a lie, which as a Christian he couldn't tolerate. So after much deliberation and prayer, he decided to take the train to Chicago and face the charges against him.

When Ron appeared in criminal court, I was there working as a reporter for the *Chicago Tribune.* In contrast to the other defendants, who were always offering excuses for their behavior, Ron looked into the judge's eyes and said, "I'm guilty. I did it. I'm responsible. If I need to go to prison, that's okay. But I've become a Christian and the right thing to do is to admit what I've done and to ask for forgiveness. What I did was wrong, plain and simple, and I'm sorry. I really am."

I was blown away! Even as an atheist, I was so impressed by what Ron did that he didn't need to approach me to talk about his faith. *I* asked *him* about it.

Over a cup of coffee, Ron recounted his entire story as I scribbled notes. Frankly, his tale was so amazing that I needed to corroborate it. I interviewed his coworkers, friends, and pastor in Oregon, as well as the street-toughened detectives who knew him in Chicago. They were unanimous in saying that something had dramatically transformed him. Ron claimed God was responsible. Though a skeptic, I was thoroughly intrigued.

Ron expected to spend two decades behind bars, away from his wife and little girl. But the judge, deeply impressed by Ron's changed life, concluded that he wasn't a threat to society anymore and gave him probation instead. "Go home and be with your family," he said.

I had never seen anything like this! After court was adjourned, I rushed into the hallway to interview Ron. "What's your reaction to what the judge did?" I asked.

Ron faced me squarely and looked deep into my eyes. "What that judge did was show me grace—sort of like Jesus did," Ron replied. "And Lee, can I tell you something? *If you let him, God will show you grace, too.* Don't forget that."

I never have. Hearing Ron tell me the story of God's transforming work in his life helped pry open my heart to God. Without a doubt, Ron Bronski was one of the key influences in my journey toward faith. Today, more than thirty years later, Ron is pastor of a church near Portland—and we're still friends.

What did Ron do that was so effective in reaching out to me? He simply lived out his faith and then told me his story. Granted, his was an amazing account. But every follower of Jesus has a story to tell. And here's a counterintuitive secret: you don't need a dramatic account in order for your testimony to influence someone for Christ.

In fact, sometimes the more mundane stories are the most effective. After all, not many people can relate to the story of a street gang leader turned pastor. But chances are that a lot of folks can identify with a story like yours.

What does Ron Bronski's story tell us about the breadth and depth of God's love?

Is there someone in your life who seems too far from God to ever come to him? What does Ron's story—and, for that matter, Lee's story—tell you about what God could do in your friend's life?

What steps could you take this week, with renewed vision, to reach out to that person or persons in order to share what God has done for you? What could God do for them?

When you consider God's grace in the lives of people like Ron Bronski, Lee Strobel, yourself, and others in your group, don't you feel moved to express your gratitude for his immeasurable love and grace? Take a moment to give him thanks and worship him.

Note

1. Greg Laurie, *Tell Someone: You Can Share the Good News* (Nashville, Tenn.: B&H Publishing Group, 2016), p. 82.

BACKING UP THE BIBLICAL RECORD OF CHRIST

Since I myself have carefully investigated everything from the beginning,
I too decided to write an orderly account for you . . .
so that you may know the certainty of the things you have been taught.

LUKE 1:3–4

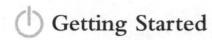 Getting Started

Welcome back to session three of *Making Your Case for Christ*. Let's take a few moments to catch up with each other, meet anyone who is new to the group, and open in prayer. Also, before we dive into our topic for today, do you have a story about sharing your testimony with someone this past week? How did it go? Does anyone want to share thoughts or lessons you gained during your *between-sessions* personal study time?

Opening Discussion

As Christians, we have strong reasons to believe what we believe—reasons that can give us a confident faith in Christ. But we don't have complete answers to every question or absolute proof that everything we believe is true—nor does any other worldview. What we *do* have is strong evidence that our beliefs are based on real facts of history, that they make sense logically, and that the Holy Spirit has given us an internal assurance that the basic tenets of our faith are true. We're going to look into some of those facts today.

"For we did not follow cleverly devised stories when we told you about the coming of our Lord Jesus Christ in power, but we were eyewitnesses of his majesty." — 2 Peter 1:16

But in the process of learning about this information and gaining a sense of spiritual confidence, it is natural to run up against what Lee Strobel likes to call "spiritual sticking points"—intellectual challenges that cause us to question or doubt our faith. These are matters that must not be ignored. Instead, we need to study diligently, trusting that, as Jesus put it in John 8:32, "You will know the truth, and the truth will set you free."

• Can you share about a "spiritual sticking point" you've wrestled with in the past—or perhaps are working through right now? What have you done or are doing to try to resolve it?

• One of the prominent spiritual sticking points in our culture is the question of whether we can know for certain that the biblical record about Jesus is accurate and reliable. Has that question come up in your interactions with family or friends? Or have any of you struggled with some aspect of that issue yourselves? What have you done to get answers in this area?

In today's teaching, Lee and Mark will talk about spiritual sticking points and the question of how we can know—and share with our friends—reasons to trust in the historical reliability of the biblical record about Jesus.

▶ Video Teaching

Watch the video for session three, in which Lee and Mark discuss the topic: "Backing Up the Biblical Record of Christ." As you watch, use the following outline to record any thoughts that stand out to you.

Opening Vignette

Some people may reach a point where, if they don't get good answers to address the doubts and questions they have about the reliability of their beliefs, they will just throw out their faith altogether. It is crucial for us to be able to back up the biblical record of Christ and to articulate our reasons to others.

Opening Teaching

Many people have spiritual "sticking points" in their lives. If they can just get good information that helps them address those issues, they can make great progress toward trusting in Christ.

A common sticking point in our culture is the question of whether or not the Bible is *reliable*. People want to know if what they read about Jesus in the New Testament is true to what really happened 2,000 years ago.

Movie Clip

Notice the powerful information that the archaeologist/priest presents to Lee regarding the manuscript evidence we have that supports the reliability of the New Testament.

Main Teaching

A good way to remember and share the evidence for the reliability of the Gospel records about Jesus is by learning five words that begin with each of the five vowels: *A, E, I, O,* and *U:*

A— _____ —reasons we can trust that the Gospels were written by those who were traditionally listed as the authors: Matthew, Mark, Luke, and John.

E— _____ _____ —evidence that the Gospels were written within a relatively short time-span after Jesus' earthly ministry, and circulated within the lifetimes of the eyewitnesses.

I— _____ of the _____ —evidence that we have early manuscripts, in great number, that support the reliability of the biblical accounts we read today.

O— _____ _____ —confirmation of the contours of the biblical record from archaeology and secular history.

U— _____ —reasons we can trust the biblical Gospels while rejecting the later alternative gospels.

Video Wrap

Using the **A-E-I-O-U** framework can help us make our case for Christ and show others that we have good reasons to trust the biblical record about him.

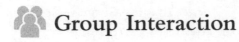 Group Interaction

In light of Lee's explanation of the evidence for the reliability of the biblical record about Jesus, take a few minutes to discuss the following questions as a group:

- Which point of the **A-E-I-O-U** outline did you find most compelling? Why?

- Was there any part of the outline that you found confusing and that you need clarified?

- Which of the objections mentioned in the teaching have you encountered in your interactions with others?

- Do you think some of the answers you heard will help you in those discussions? Which ones?

Group Reflection

Take a few minutes to scan through the summaries of the **A-E-I-O-U** points below. After reviewing those summaries, pair up with one other person and explain to each other what you consider to be the high points of each element of this framework. (Note that this will take the bulk of the remaining time in this session.)

Authorship

The challenge often presented to us is that the four Gospels—Matthew, Mark, Luke, and John—were written by unknown authors, so we can't trust them. The truth? We have good reasons, including the historical writings of the early church fathers Papias and Irenaeus, to believe the Gospels were written by the very people we've traditionally thought they were written by:

- *Matthew*, a former tax collector and an apostle of Jesus—and therefore an eyewitness to the events he records.

- *Mark,* a scribe for Peter, who wrote under the authority of a key eye-witness and leading apostle.

- *Luke,* a traveling companion of Paul, who wrote under Paul's apostolic authority. Luke assures us at the beginning of his Gospel that he "carefully investigated everything from the beginning," so when you read his account, you can "know the certainty of the things you have been taught" (Luke 1:3–4).

- *John,* "the disciple whom Jesus loved" (a phrase repeated throughout his Gospel), which history indicates was probably the young eyewitness and apostle named John.

Here's a key fact: never in history have any of the Gospels been attributed to anyone but their traditional authors. The uniform testimony of the early church is that Matthew, Mark, Luke, and John wrote the books that now bear their names.

Early Writings

The challenge we often hear related to this area is that the Gospel accounts of Jesus were written too far after the events to be considered reliable. The truth? The Gospels were written much closer to the time of Jesus than many people suppose.

How do we know? Here's one way. Start with the book of Acts, which was written by Luke, and work backward to the death and resurrection of Jesus (which happened about AD 30 or 33). Acts tells the story of Paul's conversion and his subsequent work as a missionary for the church. But it ends abruptly with Paul living under house arrest in Rome. So, Acts must have been written before Paul was executed in the early 60s. Because of this, most scholars date the book of Acts before AD 62.

> *"Any time gaps where there was only a verbal record of Jesus' teachings is becoming incredibly small — especially when compared to many other ancient biographies, which were often written centuries after the lives of those they chronicled."*

But Acts was the second of two works by Luke, with the Gospel of Luke being the first. We also know that Luke draws some of his material from Mark, which therefore must have been written prior to Luke. This puts Mark, which is generally considered the earliest of the four Gospels, back to at least the year AD 60, if not into the 50s. We also have good reason to believe the passion narrative in Mark was drawn from earlier sources—from as early as the 30s.

And Paul's letters were written even earlier than the Gospels. As we'll explore more deeply in the next session, in one of those letters Paul records an early creed of the church that many scholars believe goes back to within *months* of the life and ministry of Jesus. It details the death, resurrection, and later appearances of Jesus (see 1 Corinthians 15:3–7).

So, any time gaps where there was only a verbal record of Jesus' teachings is becoming incredibly small—especially when compared to many other ancient biographies, which were often written centuries after the lives of those whom they chronicled.

Integrity of the Text

The charge critics level is that we don't have the original writings of the Gospels but only copies. Therefore, they reason, many errors must have been introduced over the centuries by the copyists who inevitably made mistakes—making it impossible to know what the original versions actually said. The truth? As with *all* ancient writings, the materials the authors wrote on didn't last forever, but eventually crumbled into dust. People knew this would happen, which is why they worked so hard to make accurate manuscript copies of important works.

But here's what's exciting: as the movie clip illustrated, we have far more handwritten copies of the New Testament than of any other ancient book. In fact, we have more than 5,800 copies of early Greek manuscripts, and about 20,000 more in other languages. This is exponentially more manuscripts than we have for other ancient writings, and we have copies that are much earlier as well.

New Testament scholar Daniel B. Wallace explains it like this: "The average classical author's literary remains number no more than twenty copies. We have more than 1,000 times the manuscript data for the New Testament than we do for the average Greco-Roman author. Not only this, but the extant manuscripts of the average classical author are no earlier than 500 years after the time he wrote. For the New Testament, we are waiting mere decades for surviving copies."[1]

Summing up, when we compare the wealth of manuscript evidence for the New Testament to other ancient writings, we have, as Wallace puts it, "an embarrassment of riches."

"We have more than 1,000 times the manuscript data for the New Testament than we do for the average Greco-Roman author. Not only this, but the extant manuscripts of the average classical author are no earlier than 500 years after the time he wrote. For the New Testament, we are waiting mere decades for surviving copies." — Daniel B. Wallace

---

Outside Corroboration

We often hear the Gospels shouldn't be trusted because they report things secular history and archaeology don't confirm. For example, critics have claimed there was no city of Nazareth in the first century, so therefore Jesus could not have grown up where the Gospels say he did.

The truth? In 2006, British archaeologists excavated beneath the Sisters of Nazareth Convent and discovered a house there from the first century. They also found limestone pottery, which Jewish families were known to use during that time. And then, three years later, they found another house that was also dated to that same era. In short, the archaeological evidence backed up the biblical record.

This has happened over and over again. Skeptics doubted the existence of Pilate, the Roman governor who tried Jesus. But then a first-century plaque was unearthed that had Pilate's name inscribed on it, referring to him as "Pontius Pilate, Prefect of Judea." They also challenged the Gospel of Luke, because in Luke 3:1 he refers to Lysanias as the tetrarch of Abilene in about AD 27. For years, critics scoffed because Lysanias was not the tetrarch but a king who had been executed fifty years earlier. But then an inscription was found from the time of Tiberius (AD 14–37) declaring that Lysanias *was* tetrarch in Abila near Damascus, just as Luke had claimed. It turns out there were two Lysaniases—and, again, the Gospel account was proven correct through archaeological research.

In fact, here's what we can know about Jesus from purely non-biblical, non-Christian ancient sources, without even consulting the Bible: Jesus was a Jewish teacher; many believed he performed healings and exorcisms; some believed he was the Messiah; he was rejected by Jewish leaders; he was crucified under Pontius Pilate during the reign of Tiberius; despite this shameful death, his followers, who believed he was still alive, spread beyond Palestine so there were multitudes of them in Rome by AD 64, and all kinds of people from the cities and the countryside, men and women, slave and free, worshiped him as God.

Uniqueness

The challenge here is that a number of alternative Gospels have been discovered in recent years—such as the Gospel of Thomas, the Gospel of Judas, the Gospel of Mary, the Secret Gospel of Mark, the Gospel of Peter, and others—and these tell a different story than we read in the four biblical Gospels. Further, the skeptic will contend, these other gospels should be treated as equals to Matthew, Mark, Luke, and John.

The truth? Yes, there are numerous other "gospels" that have been discovered since 1945, but none of them have the same first-century eyewitness credentials as the Gospels in the Bible. Generally, they come about 100 years or more *after* the real Gospels. Therefore, none of them are connected to the people whose names are associated with them.

"That which was from the beginning, which we have heard, which we have seen with our eyes, which we have looked at . . . this we proclaim concerning the Word of life." — 1 John 1:1

Take, for example, the Gospel of Thomas, which claims to be a collection of 114 "hidden" sayings of Jesus. But Thomas was written in about AD 175–200—roughly a century too late to be related to the real apostle Thomas—and is infected by gnostic teaching that runs contrary to the teachings of the Bible. The Gospel of Thomas presents a different gospel, saying that salvation comes from understanding oneself authentically and recognizing where one fits into the cosmos, as well as repudiating this world. But that's not the biblical message.

Further, the Gospel of Thomas is full of strange teachings. For example, it quotes Simon Peter as saying, "Let Mary go away from us because women are not worthy of life." And it reports Jesus as saying, "I shall lead her in order to make her a male, so that she too may become a living spirit, resembling you males. For every woman who makes herself male will enter into the kingdom of heaven." Does that sound like *anything* the real Jesus said?

Then there's this statement: "If you fast, you will bring sin upon yourselves, and if you pray, you will be condemned, and if you give to charity, you will harm your spirits." And finally, "Blessings on the lion if a human eats it, making the lion human. Foul is the human if a lion eats it, making the lion human." *What?*

The deeper you look into this challenge, the clearer the answer becomes: none of the other so-called "gospels" have the credibility or the authentic content of the true, biblical Gospels of Matthew, Mark, Luke, and John.

> *"The evidence is clear: none of the other so-called 'gospels' have the credibility or the authentic content of the true, biblical Gospels of Matthew, Mark, Luke, and John."*

 # Conclusion

New Testament scholar Craig A. Evans summed up the evidence well when he said, "There's every reason to conclude that the Gospels have fairly and accurately reported the essential elements of Jesus' teachings, life, death, and resurrection. They're early enough, they're rooted into the right streams that go back to Jesus and the original people, there's continuity, there's proximity, there's verification of certain distinct points with archaeology and other documents, and then there's the inner logic."[2]

Now that we've reviewed some of the information that backs up the biblical record about Christ using the **A-E-I-O-U** outline, let's add one more element from the additional part-time vowel: *"and sometimes Y."*

Y—*You and Your friends* can be confident that the biblical record for Christ is early, reliable, and well preserved—and therefore worthy of your trust!

Closing Challenge

This week, deepen your understanding of the evidence that backs up the gospel record of Christ by reviewing the summary of the **A-E-I-O-U** outline on pages 52–57. This information is best mastered by repetition as well as by telling others what you've learned.

For more information, read *The Case for Christ* by Lee Strobel, especially Part 1, "Examining the Record." Also, read *In Defense of Jesus* by Lee Strobel, especially the sections on Challenge #1 and Challenge #2.

Look for opportunities this week to talk to friends who might have questions in this area and to put to work some of the information you've learned today. Be ready to share stories of any conversations you have when we're together next time. Also be sure to come back for the next session, when we'll address another vitally important subject: "Presenting Evidence for the Resurrection of Christ."

Finishing the Session

Let's close in prayer, thanking God for the solid information that backs up the biblical record of Christ and asking for opportunities to share this information— and our faith in general—with the people in our lives.

BETWEEN-SESSIONS
PERSONAL STUDY

Reflect on the content we've covered this week in *Making Your Case for Christ* by engaging in the following *between-sessions* activities. The time you invest will serve to enhance your confidence in the biblical record and help prepare you to share what you've learned with others. At the next meeting there will be time for you to tell your group about any insights you've gained.

Study God's Word

While we have broad historical and archaeological evidence to support the validity of the Bible, it's also helpful to know what the biblical writers themselves have said about their process of writing what God revealed to them. In the following section, we'll examine three passages related to this topic, followed by three reflection questions under each passage.

John

In 1 John 1:1–3, John wrote, "That which was from the beginning, which we have heard, which we have seen with our eyes, which we have looked at and our hands have touched—this we proclaim concerning the Word of life. The life appeared; we have seen it and testify to it, and we proclaim to you the eternal life, which was with the Father and has appeared to us. We proclaim to you what we have seen and heard, so that you also may have fellowship with us."

It is often claimed that the biblical record was written down after many years of oral tradition had been passed from person to person. Do you see anything like that in what John explains in this passage? Where did he get his information?

Sometimes people will say biblical claims about Christ were based on ethereal spiritual experiences that should not be taken as literal truths. Does John seem to be describing some kind of a mystical experience here? How many times does he mention his various senses being involved in his very real encounters with Jesus, the "Word of life"?

Seeing that John wrote his accounts out of such rich and personal experience with the Son of God, what affect does that have on you when you read his words?

Luke

Luke starts his Gospel with this explanation: "Many have undertaken to draw up an account of the things that have been fulfilled among us, just as they were handed down to us by those who from the first were eyewitnesses and servants of the word. With this in mind, since I myself have carefully investigated everything from the beginning, I too decided to write an orderly account for you, most excellent Theophilus, so that you may know the certainty of the things you have been taught" (Luke 1:1–4).

Luke indicates he was not an eyewitness of Jesus or the events surrounding his ministry, but he makes it clear he gained his information from eyewitnesses and "carefully investigated everything from the beginning."

Lee Strobel calls Luke a "first-century investigative reporter." After reading Luke's approach to putting together his biography of Jesus, how reliable do you think it was? How does that impact your attitude in sharing it with others?

In order for a Gospel or an Epistle to be included in the New Testament collection of writings (the New Testament canon), it had to be written by an apostle who was an eyewitness or under the authority of one. Luke was not an apostle, so where did he get the authority to write the Gospel of Luke and the book of Acts? (Hint: If you read Acts 16:10 and the verses that follow it, you'll see Luke describing how "we" were traveling here and there—including himself and which apostle?)

Luke finished his opening passage by saying he went through the painstaking process of checking things carefully, "so that you may know the certainty of the things you have been taught." How does that bolster your confidence in sharing the story of Jesus with the people you hope to reach for him?

Peter

Peter wrote, "Above all, you must understand that no prophecy of Scripture came about by the prophet's own interpretation of things. For prophecy never had its origin in the human will, but prophets, though human, spoke from God as they were carried along by the Holy Spirit" (2 Peter 1:20–21).

Another challenge we often hear is that the Bible is just a human book, written by men—so why treat it as being any more important than any other human book? How do Peter's words challenge that assumption?

We see a variety of human personalities and writing styles in the pages of Scripture, but Peter says that "no prophecy of Scripture came about by the prophet's own interpretation of things." What does this mean to you on a practical level?

It is hard to enthusiastically promote an idea to your friends that you're not fully convinced of yourself. When you combine the varieties of evidence we reviewed in this session with the strong claims of the biblical writers, don't you feel a growing confidence in the validity of what you believe? Which aspects of this information do you think would be most helpful to share with your friends who don't yet know Christ?

Put It into Practice

Now that you've studied the claims of a few of the biblical writers, as well as some of the supporting historical evidence for the Scriptures, how would you respond if one of your friends raised the following objections?

"Nobody really knows who wrote the New Testament—but whoever it was, they were simply writing down ideas that had been passed around by word of mouth."

"You can't trust the so-called historical record about Jesus because it was written down so long after he died that it's impossible to sort out fact from fiction."

"Even if the biblical writers got their stories more or less straight about Jesus, their writings have been obscured through centuries of copies being made of copies, so we can no longer trust anything that we have in our possession today."

"The Bible is written by a bunch of believers who have talked each other into thinking it's true. Well, it's a nice story—but it's not supported by real history."

"There were lots of early biographies written about Jesus. Why should we accept the Gospels of Matthew or John over and above the Gospels of Judas or Thomas?"

Reflect on a Key Story

The following is an inspiring story Mark Mittelberg tells in *The Unexpected Adventure* about some skeptical students that he and Lee Strobel were able to help years ago. Their questions about Christianity included the one we explored in this session concerning the reliability of the biblical record. Take a few minutes to read it, and then consider your responses to the questions that follow it.

Making Room for Questions

Mark Mittelberg

"I used to be a Christian."

Those were the first words out of the young man's mouth. We'd never met before, but he had called because someone told him I would take his spiritual questions seriously. His opening line grabbed my full attention. As our telephone conversation went on, I soon realized that I was his final recourse in a last-ditch effort to get some answers before permanently abandoning his faith.

"Look, these issues you're raising are serious. I don't want to offer quick-fix answers over the phone," I told him. "How about coming to my office so we can sit down and really work through some of your questions?"

He seemed surprised. "You'd be willing to do that?"

"Of course I would. When can you come in?" I replied, surprised that he was surprised by my willingness to meet when so much was at stake. We lined up an appointment, and when the time came, he arrived with a friend who, I quickly found out, had many of the same spiritual roadblocks.

As their story unfolded, I learned that they had been part of a nearby congregation that was fairly authoritarian in its approach. The church declared the truth and expected its members to accept it—no questions asked. The problem was that my two high school friends *did* have questions, and they kept asking them.

The first time they raised their objections during a class at church, their teacher shut them down. "Those are things that people of faith must accept *by faith*," he insisted. "You just need to believe, and then you'll know that it's true."

To my friends—as well as to me—this sounded like an admission that there are no good reasons to believe, so you just have to accept it as part of a blind leap in the dark. Kind of like saying, "Leap before you look; you might get lucky."

When I asked how they handled that encounter, they told me they tried to comply, but their doubts only grew. Later that summer they had gone to their church camp, where they had a different set of leaders. They decided to give it another try, but once again the people in charge silenced them. "You must not raise these issues here," they warned. "You'll only confuse the other campers."

So they held in their questions while their doubts continued to fester, poisoning their faith.

"Then what did you do?" I asked, trying not to let out my real feelings about how they had been so horribly mishandled.

"Well, we finally decided that the Bible couldn't be trusted and that the Christian faith teaches things it can't prove. So we basically abandoned our belief in God," they said.

As disturbing as that was, what I heard next just about knocked me out of my chair.

"And this fall we changed what had been our weekly Bible study into a 'Skeptics Group.' It's a place where we invite our friends from school to come hear the evidence *against* the Bible and Christianity."

"That's … fascinating," I said, trying to stay calm. "So what made you come and tell me all of this?"

"A friend challenged us, saying that before we go any further we ought to slow down and test our thinking one more time. He gave us your name and said you might be able to help us out."

"Well, I'm really glad you're here, and I'm willing to do whatever it takes to help you get answers to your objections," I said, hoping to encourage them with good information as well as my personal interest. "I also want to tell you up front that I'm confident in the truth of Christianity and anxious to discuss whatever has been hurting your faith."

With that, we launched into a three-hour conversation about their main areas of concern, which included many of the standard objections about why God allows evil and suffering, questions about the reliability of the Bible, and problems with hypocrisy among religious people—both past and present. By no means easy issues, but certainly not new ones either.

By the end of that discussion, I could tell that their doubts were beginning to dissolve. But what came next got me even more excited.

"Before we go, can I make a request?"

"Sure. What is it?"

"I was wondering if you'd be willing to come to our next Skeptics Group meeting at my house to explain some of this information to the rest of our friends. I think they'd be interested in what you have to say."

"Yes," I said, not needing more than a nanosecond to think about it. "When do you meet?" He gave me the details, and I asked him one more question: "When I invited you to meet with me today, you brought a friend with you, which is great. Now you're inviting me to come and meet with you; would it be okay if I bring a friend with me?"

"Of course," he answered.

We said good-bye until the next time we would see each other at the upcoming Skeptics Group.

The following week I went to his house, bringing with me Lee—*"The Case for Christ"*—Strobel. We had a grand time talking for hours with this circle of sincere but spiritually confused teenagers, sharing our testimonies, answering their questions, and challenging their thinking.

God really worked during our time together, so much so that by the end of the evening the original student had recommitted his life to Christ. And within two weeks the friend he had brought to my office became a believer.

Then together they converted their Skeptics Group back into a bona fide Bible study and started reaching out to their friends at school, showing them the truths that support their faith and encouraging them to follow Jesus, just as they were now doing.

All because someone was willing to make room for questions.

Does this story raise your sense of urgency to "be prepared to give an answer to everyone who asks you to give the reason for the hope that you have" (1 Peter 3:15)? What else can you do to be better prepared?

Young people are especially vulnerable to intellectual attacks. Are there any students in your life who God might be leading you to reach out to in order to teach and encourage them in their faith?

These students found it frustrating to be shut down when they were just trying to ask questions about what they had been taught. What can you do to let people around you know their questions matter and that you're excited to help them find answers? Is there anything that you could do to address this need on a church-wide level?

We have primarily focused on the questions and doubts of others. But are there areas that trouble *you* or sometimes cause you to doubt your faith? Who can you turn to for help on this matter? What book should you read? (You might want to check the *For Further Reading* section at the end of this study guide for some ideas.)

Notes

1. Justin Taylor, "An Interview with Daniel B. Wallace on the New Testament Manuscripts," The Gospel Coalition, March 22, 2012. https://www.thegospelcoalition.org/blogs/justin-taylor/an-interview-with-daniel-b-wallace-on-the-new-testament-manuscripts/.
2. Craig A. Evans, quoted in Lee Strobel, *In Defense of Jesus: Investigating Attacks on the Identity of Christ* (Grand Rapids, Mich.: Zondervan, 2016).

PRESENTING EVIDENCE FOR THE RESURRECTION OF CHRIST

For what I received I passed on to you as of first importance: that Christ died for our sins according to the Scriptures, that he was buried, that he was raised on the third day according to the Scriptures, and that he appeared to Cephas, and then to the Twelve. After that, he appeared to more than five hundred . . . at the same time.

1 CORINTHIANS 15:3–6

Getting Started

Welcome back to session four of *Making Your Case for Christ*. Today we're going to talk about the evidence for the central, make-or-break claim of the Christian faith: that Jesus rose from the dead. But first let's take a moment to hear any stories about conversations you might have had this past week about the topics we've been discussing. Also, briefly reviewing last week's discussion about the reliability of the biblical record of Christ, can you recite the words represented by the letters **A-E-I-O-U**?

Opening Discussion

Anyone who reads the New Testament knows Jesus made a lot of serious claims about who he was and what he came to do. He communicated he was the long-awaited Messiah (see John 4:25–26), the unique Son of God who shares the divine nature of the Father (see John 5:16–18), the loving Savior who came to "give his life as a ransom for many" (Mark 10:45), and the Son of Man who would someday return on the clouds of heaven (see Mark 14:62 and Daniel 7:13–14).

> *"I am the resurrection and the life. The one who believes in me will live, even though they die." — John 11:25*

In short, Jesus claimed to be the eternal God in human flesh, who came to earth with the express purpose of dying for our sins so he could freely offer us salvation and eternity in heaven. The apostles repeatedly reinforced these same truths (see, for example, Philippians 2:5–11). But how can we know that Jesus' claims were really true?

Many answers could be given, including the fact that Jesus was born where it was predicted the Messiah would be born (in Bethlehem; see Micah 5:2), that he fulfilled many other Old Testament prophecies about the Messiah (see Psalm 22; Isaiah 7:14; 9:1–2, 9:6; 53:1–12; and numerous other passages), that he did an array of amazing miracles (see John 10:37–38), and that he lived a sinless life (see 1 Peter 2:22–23; 1 John 3:5).

But beyond any of these, Jesus answered this question when the religious leaders pressed him for a miraculous sign in order to prove who he was. He answered them by saying that, at least in their case, "None will be given except the sign of the prophet Jonah. For as Jonah was three days and three nights in the belly of a huge fish, so the Son of Man will be three days and three nights in the heart of the earth" (Matthew 12:39–40). In other words, Jesus predicted that after his coming execution, he would be in the grave only three days before rising from the dead—and *that* would be the proof they were looking for.

- The apostle Paul added in 1 Corinthians 15:14, "If Christ has not been raised, our preaching is useless and so is your faith." Why is that the case?

- How does Jesus' death and resurrection set him apart from the founders of the other religions?

In this session's teaching, Lee and Mark will discuss details of the evidence related to Jesus' resurrection.

⏵ Video Teaching

Watch the video for session four, in which Lee and Mark discuss "Presenting Evidence for the Resurrection of Christ." As you watch, use the following outline to record any concepts that stand out to you.

Opening Vignette

Anyone can *claim* to be God, but if Jesus *actually* rose from the dead, that's good evidence he is telling the truth. This is why the resurrection is the proverbial "ball game" when it comes to making our case for faith in Christ.

Opening Teaching

Jesus claimed to be the divine Son of God. He came claiming he was going to give his life as payment for humanity's sins. He banked everything on the resurrection.

Movie Clip

In the first scene, watch how the actor who plays the part of Gary Habermas—one of the leading scholars in the world on the resurrection—presents reasons we can be confident Jesus really did rise from the dead.

In the second scene, notice how the world-famous psychologist explained to Lee why it didn't make sense to say the disciples merely had hallucinations or visions of the risen Jesus.

Main Teaching

A good way to present the evidence for the resurrection of Jesus is by using what Lee called "the Four *E*'s":

    First E: _____—we can know that Jesus actually died on the cross when he was crucified by the Romans.

Second E: _____ _____—we can know the resurrection of Jesus wasn't a myth or legend that developed centuries after he died.

Ancient Creed:

Saul of Tarsus:

Third E: _____ _____—we can know that Jesus' body was missing.

Jerusalem Factor:

Criterion of Embarrassment:

Enemy Attestation:

Fourth E: _____—we can know that Jesus actually appeared to a number of different individuals in a variety of settings after his resurrection.

Witness of the disciples:

James and Paul:

Video Wrap

The Four *E*'s create a clear, compelling, and persuasive case for the fact that Jesus not only *claimed* to be God but he *backed it up* by rising from the dead.

 # Group Interaction

There was a lot of important information in this teaching that can help reinforce our confidence in the reality of Jesus' resurrection. Take a few minutes to consider the points that were made and to discuss the following questions as a group:

- Which of the Four *E*'s was the least familiar to you?

- Did any of the points Lee made surprise you or strike you in a fresh way?

- Which point or points do you think will be the strongest for the people you talk to about spiritual matters? Why?

- Is there a point or two that you want to study up on a bit more?

Group Reflection

Now let's take a few minutes to review and highlight the key points related to the Four *E*'s of Jesus' resurrection. You can go back to any notes you took above, but let's also take a few minutes to scan the summaries of the main points below. Then pair up with one other person and take turns summarizing the Four *E*'s to each other, allowing time for review as well as interaction with each other. (Note that this will take the bulk of the remaining time in this session.)

Execution

Jesus died when he was crucified, and there is no record of anyone ever surviving a full Roman crucifixion. He was beaten dozens of times with whips that had jagged bones and balls of lead woven into them. The historian Eusebius described such a flogging: "The sufferer's veins were laid bare, and the very muscles, sinews, and bowels of the victim were open to exposure." Then, while Jesus was in hypovolemic shock, the spikes were driven through his wrists and feet, and he was hung on the cross. Crucifixion results in slow asphyxiation because stress on the chest locks the person's lungs into an inhaled position.

After Jesus "breathed his last," a soldier plunged a spear between his ribs, puncturing his heart, and proving that he was indeed dead.[1] "Clearly the weight of the historical and medical evidence indicates that Jesus was dead before the wound to his side was inflicted," researchers concluded in the *Journal of the American Medical Association*.[2]

> *"Clearly the weight of the historical and medical evidence indicates that Jesus was dead before the wound to his side was inflicted." — Journal of the American Medical Association*

Each of the four Gospels, written early and rooted in eyewitness accounts, make it clear that Jesus died on the cross (see Matthew 27:45–56; Mark 15:33–41; Luke 23:44–49; John 19:28–37). Atheist Gerd Lüdemann summed up the evidence well: "Jesus' death as a consequence of crucifixion is indisputable."[3]

Early Accounts

The written records of Jesus' death and resurrection are early and reliable. It was once common for critics to claim that the Gospels—Matthew, Mark, Luke, and John—were written too late to give us accurate information about the life of Jesus, including his resurrection. However, as we saw in the last session, it is now known that the Gospels—and the entire New Testament—were written in the first century, and within the lifespan of Jesus' followers.

Even before the Gospels were recorded, Paul penned his epistles. These letters affirm many details about Jesus' life, including his resurrection. In addition, Paul's letters relay several earlier creeds, including the one in 1 Corinthians 15:3–7. Historian Gary Habermas developed a helpful timeline related to this creed. It starts with understanding that Jesus was crucified in either AD 30 or 33. Paul wrote 1 Corinthians in about AD 54–55, which puts it within approximately twenty-one to twenty-five years of the crucifixion.

But we can go even earlier. Paul said in 1 Corinthians 15:3, "What I received I passed on to you." When did he receive it? He became a Christian one to three years after Jesus' execution and immediately went into Damascus and met with some of the apostles. Many historians believe this is when he was given the creed. Others say he got it in Jerusalem when he met with Peter and James three years later. Both of them are named in the creed as eyewitnesses to the risen Jesus (Paul mentions his visit with them in Galatians 1:18–19). This means Paul was given the creed within one to six years of the crucifixion—and it had already been put into creedal form, which tells us these beliefs went back even further.

"This tradition," concluded historian James D. G. Dunn, "we can be entirely confident, was *formulated as tradition within months of Jesus' death*."[4] And this creed was just one early report—the accounts in Matthew, Mark, Luke, John, and Acts date back so early that they were circulated within the lifetimes of Jesus' contemporaries, who would have pointed out any errors if they had been making up the story.

*"We don't have a huge time gap between the death of Jesus and the development of a legend saying he rose from the dead. We have a **newsflash** from ancient history that goes back to the beginning."*

Empty Tomb

According to the earliest accounts, Jesus' body was laid in a tomb belonging to Joseph of Arimathea. The tomb was sealed and placed under guard—and yet, it was discovered empty on Easter morning by the women and later by Peter and John. In his book *How Jesus Became God*, agnostic author Bart Ehrman tries to cast doubt on Jesus being buried in a tomb. He writes, "If the Romans followed their normal policies and customs, and if Pilate was the man whom all our sources indicate he was, then it is highly unlikely that Jesus was decently buried on the day of his execution in a tomb that anyone could later identify."[5]

But in *How God Became Jesus*, Craig Evans said Ehrman's analysis of Roman policy on crucifixion and burial is unnuanced and incomplete. He makes a compelling case that "the Gospel accounts describing Jesus' removal from the cross and burial are consistent with archaeological evidence and with Jewish law." Evans adds that it is "simply erroneous to assert Romans did not permit the burial of the executed, including the crucified."[6]

We have archaeological evidence that crucifixion victims were buried. A buried crucifixion victim from the first century was unearthed in 1968 with a seven-inch nail driven into his feet and olive wood from his cross still attached. And scores of nails bearing calcium from human bones were discovered in tombs from that era.

What other evidence do we have pointing to the tomb being empty? First, *the Jerusalem Factor*. Scholar William Lane Craig points out that the site of Jesus' tomb was known to Christians and non-Christians alike. If it were not empty, it would have been impossible for a new religious movement founded on the resurrection to explode in the same city where Jesus was publicly executed.[7]

Second, the *Criterion of Embarrassment*. It was women who found the empty tomb. But according to the Talmud, "Any evidence which a woman [gives] is not valid (to offer)." And Jewish historian Josephus said, "But let not the testimony of women be admitted." So the fact that the first witnesses of the empty tomb were women would have been an embarrassing part of the story in that culture and weakened their case. But that's the kind of embarrassing detail that historians see as an earmark of truth—because if you were just making up stories, you wouldn't have included such a detail. New Testament scholar Craig A. Evans concludes, "In my view the tradition of the women as first discoverers is a strong piece of evidence in favor of the historicity of the empty tomb, if not the reality of the resurrection also."[8]

Third, we have *Enemy Attestation*. Perhaps the strongest evidence for the empty tomb is that even Jesus' enemies implicitly admitted his tomb was vacant. Rather than refute the claims of his resurrection, they made up a cover story to explain why the body was missing (see Matthew 28:11–15). The record is clear: on that first Easter morning, Jesus' body was no longer in the tomb.

Eyewitnesses

The creed cited in 1 Corinthians 15 explains in verses 5–8 not only that Jesus' tomb was empty, but also that the risen Jesus appeared to at least 515 people, including the apostle Paul himself. In fact, when we look at the broader New Testament, we get more details of how the risen Savior appeared over a period of forty days after his resurrection to a variety of people in a variety of settings—to men and women, some individually, some in groups, sometimes indoors, sometimes outdoors, to softhearted people like John, and to skeptical people like Thomas. And at times, Jesus asked them to touch the scars in his hands or side, or to eat with him, making it clear that he was present physically and not just spiritually.

"[After Jesus' resurrection] he appeared to Cephas, and then to the Twelve. After that, he appeared to more than five hundred of the brothers and sisters at the same time. . . . Then he appeared to James, then to all the apostles, and last of all he appeared to me also." — 1 Corinthians 15:5—8

What's more, these reports come from multiple sources, both inside and outside the New Testament. Historian Michael Licona summarized, "In all, we've got nine sources that reflect multiple, very early, and eyewitness testimonies to the disciples' claims that they had seen the risen Jesus. This is something the disciples believed to the core of their being."[9]

The evidence is so strong that atheist scholar Gerd Lüdemann said, "It may be taken as historically certain that Peter and the disciples had experiences after Jesus' death in which Jesus appeared to them as the risen Christ."[10]

Could these appearances have actually been hallucinations? As we saw in the movie clip, the hallucination hypothesis is not possible because, like dreams, these are individual events that can't be shared. Yet we have reports of Jesus appearing several times to multiple people at once, including 500 people as noted in the creed—and 500 people sharing the same hallucination would be a bigger miracle than the resurrection itself! In addition, if they *were* just hallucinations, Jesus' body would have still been in the tomb—but it was not.

These weren't hallucinations, visions, legends, or mistakes. They were real events of history that revolutionized lives. And the disciples were willing to die for their claims—not because they had faith, but because they were there and knew it really happened. The resurrection was the central proclamation of the early church from the very beginning. The earliest Christians didn't just endorse Jesus' teachings; they were convinced they had seen him alive after his crucifixion.

Conclusion

What we've discussed today is evidence for an event that represents really good news for those who follow Christ. He really did rise from the dead! This means:

- Jesus really was who he claimed to be—the eternal Son of God.

- His promises are true and can be trusted, including the promise of heaven for all those who follow him.

- He is alive and able to fulfill all of his promises.

Closing Challenge

Review the details of the Four *E*'s so you really understand and can explain this life-giving information to others. For more information on Jesus' resurrection, read *The Case for Christ* by Lee Strobel—especially Part 3, "Researching the Resurrection." Also read *In Defense of Jesus* by Lee Strobel, especially the sections under Challenge #3. Look for opportunities to share the Four *E*'s with someone this week—preferably someone who doesn't yet know Christ. Then tell the group how it went next time we meet. And please don't miss the next session, when we'll explore how we can clearly explain the central, life-giving message of the gospel.

Finishing the Session

Let's close in prayer, thanking God that Jesus not only died for our sins but also rose from the dead and is therefore alive to give us new life. Thank him, too, that he left lots of evidence to show us that this is all true.

Reflect on the content we've covered this week in *Making Your Case for Christ* by delving into any or all of the following *between-sessions* activities. By engaging with this material, you'll deepen your grasp on the evidence for Jesus' resurrection. At your next meeting, there will be time for you to share with your group any key points or insights that stood out to you.

📖 Study God's Word

We have talked about what the Bible says regarding the main elements of the Good Friday and Easter story, and we've quoted a few key verses here and there. But nothing can replace reading and reflecting on the primary passages of Scripture for yourself. In the following section, let's read and reflect on the sequential telling of the story in the Gospel of Luke.

The Crucifixion

Read first about the *crucifixion* of Jesus in Luke 23:26–56.

It's been said Jesus is a wedge that forces people to one side or the other: either they are for him or against him. How did this play out with the two criminals who were crucified on either side of Jesus (see verses 39–43)?

Even in the midst of the agony of his crucifixion, Jesus was dispensing grace to a penitent criminal on the cross next to him. What insights does that give you into the heart of Jesus and the mission he was on?

Recall atheist scholar Gerd Lüdemann's statement, "It may be taken as historically certain that Peter and the disciples had experiences after Jesus' death in which Jesus appeared to them as the risen Christ." When you read anew the details of the suffering of your Savior, what thoughts and emotions does it stir in you? What do you want to say to him, even now, in response to what he did for you?

The Resurrection

Now read about the *resurrection* of Jesus in Luke 24:1–12.

Jesus told his followers, multiple times, that he would suffer and die and then be raised back to life after three days. Why do you think they were still so shocked when it actually happened?

We're all in danger of reading God's clear revelation in the Bible but being slow to comprehend it or embrace it. Can you think of an example in your own situation? What could you do to more deeply grasp and accept what God is saying to you?

It's thrilling to read in this and the other biblical resurrection accounts how the followers of Jesus moved from bewilderment to an amazed belief that their Lord had risen from the grave. Take a moment to reflect on the magnitude of their realization and all it meant to them. Then ponder this question: *What does it mean to me?*

The Appearances

Finally, read about some of the *appearances* of the risen Jesus in Luke 24:13–53.

When you read about the initial discovery that the tomb was empty, as well as the accounts of some of the first appearances of the risen Jesus, you see the repeated mention that it was *women* who first made these discoveries. Why do you think that was so significant, especially in that time and culture?

In verse 25, we read that Jesus said to the two disciples on the road to Emmaus, "How foolish you are, and how slow to believe all that the prophets have spoken!" It was a gentle rebuke, followed by what must have been an amazing Bible lesson, but can you relate to these disciples' predicament? Is there something that God is trying to get through to you about but you've been slow to accept what he was saying? What can you do today to change that?

One thing is clear in all the resurrection narratives, and it carries into the accounts of the early church in the book of Acts: once people understood that Jesus had truly risen, they couldn't stop talking about it! How and where can you tell others about the exciting news that Jesus has risen (indeed!)?

 ## Put It into Practice

We've learned in this session about four points of evidence that give us confidence that Jesus truly rose from the dead. We described these as the Four *E*'s: *Execution, Early Accounts, Empty Tomb,* and *Eyewitnesses.* These are probably becoming familiar terms to you by now, but the best way to ingrain them more deeply into your awareness is to talk about them to more people. Doing so will help you know them better, and it will inform someone who needs to understand what you have now learned!

So, here's the challenge. Go back once more to the summary of the Four *E*'s, review and refresh them in your mind, and then call or contact someone you sense God leading you to share this information with. Maybe a son or daughter? Your spouse? Your parents, or perhaps a niece or nephew? Sunday school students or friends? Someone at work or in the neighborhood? At your high school or university?

Someone you know is dying to hear what you have to tell them. So take a small risk and reach out to that person right away. It could set a chain of events into motion that will stretch all the way into eternity!

 ## Reflect on a Key Story

The following is an encouraging account that Mark Mittelberg relays in *The Unexpected Adventure* about a man who didn't think he could believe in the resurrection of Christ. Take a moment to read it, and then consider your responses to the questions at the end.

The Impact of Evidence

Mark Mittelberg

"I'd *like* to become a Christian, but I still have a few questions that are hanging me up," said John Swift, a fast-talking, hard-hitting commercial banker who worked in downtown Chicago.

I was meeting with him for the first time at the request of Ernie, a leader of one of our small groups for seekers at our church, who had been dealing for some time with John's list of spiritual doubts and objections. "Let's talk about whatever is holding you back," I told John. "I hope you know you don't need to have an answer to every question in order to become a Christian."

"I realize that," he replied. "But if I'm reading you guys right, my main question deals with something you all consider to be a fairly big deal."

"Maybe or maybe not," I said. "What is it?"

Emphatically, John shot back, "I don't believe in the resurrection of Christ."

At this point I had to concede that, yes, that issue is a big deal to us in the church. "I'll admit that when I went to seminary, the resurrection of Christ fell under the heading of *biggies*. That's because the Bible clearly teaches that this is one of the truths essential to being a follower of Christ. But I'm curious, why don't you believe Jesus rose from the dead?"

"It just doesn't make sense to me that a dead person could come back to life," he explained. "Everything I've ever seen supports the fact that dead people simply stay in the grave and their bodies rot there or get eaten by wild dogs. Why should I believe it was any different for Jesus?"

It was a great question. Why should we put our faith in a claim that contradicts everything we've ever seen or experienced? Before venturing a response, I decided to ask him what he'd been doing to study the matter.

"Mostly," he replied, "I've read and listened to the scholars featured in the media."

"Which ones?" I asked, fearing the very response I was about to hear.

"I don't know all of their names," John replied, "but they're part of something called the Jesus Seminar, and I've got to tell you that those guys have all kinds of negative things to say about the idea of Jesus rising from the dead."

"I'm very aware of that," I said, sounding a bit more impatient than I'd intended. "Haven't you read any of the great books that present the actual historical evidence for the resurrection, such as the writings of Norman Geisler, Josh McDowell, or Gary Habermas?"

"Honestly, Mark, I don't know about any of their books, and I've never really heard anything that sounded like genuine evidence for Jesus' resurrection. Maybe you can fill me in."

"I'd be happy to," I replied, as we launched into an hour-plus discussion about some of the key points of evidence. The more we talked, the more encouraged I was by John's receptivity. At the same time, I was amazed and frustrated that so many spiritually inquisitive seekers are completely unaware of such vitally important information, even though it has been around for two thousand years.

The minutes flew by, and soon we were out of time. "Before you go," I said to John, "I'd like to loan you a book that I think will help deepen your understanding of the overwhelming amount of evidence that supports the resurrection."

Handing him my copy of *Jesus Under Fire*, edited by Michael Wilkins and J. P. Moreland (Zondervan, 1996), I added, "I'm sure the whole book would be helpful to you, but I'd especially like to encourage you to read through the chapter titled 'Did Jesus Rise from the Dead?' by William Lane Craig. I think it will clearly address your question."

Then I added one more thought that even surprised me. "John, I know you're a businessman who relates to challenges and goals. So let me urge you to read that chapter right away and maybe look at some of the other books I've been telling you about so you can see how strong the evidence really is. Then, assuming you confirm this to be true, I want to challenge you to become a Christian before Easter, which is only about a month away. That way you'll be able to finally celebrate the holiday for its real meaning."

The look of intensity in John's eyes told me he was taking my challenge seriously. It wasn't more than a couple of weeks later that he sent my book back with a note informing me that he'd already combed through the chapter by Bill Craig several times, read the entire book, and then went out and purchased several copies of the book for himself and a few friends who were asking similar questions. (I love it when non-Christians get involved in the adventure of evangelism.)

About two weeks later, while I was on a speaking trip in Australia, I phoned in to listen to my voicemails, and I heard a message that took my breath away.

Ernie, John's seeker small group leader, excitedly reported that John had trusted in Christ *just a few days before Easter*. When I got back home, I called John to congratulate and encourage him. Soon after, I had the privilege of baptizing him in the pond by our church.

For me, this was another vivid illustration of how God uses answers to tough questions to clear away obstacles and open a person's heart for the gospel. Through the years, I've lost count of the number of times that I've seen the Holy Spirit perform this kind of spiritual jujitsu, employing logic and evidence to turn an objection to Christianity into another reason to believe.

Notice in the story that John said, "I don't believe in the resurrection of Christ"—not, "I don't *want to* believe in the resurrection of Christ"! He actually did, in fact, want to believe, but he needed answers and information that would allow him to move forward in his journey toward faith. What lessons can you draw from that?

It's been said that "apologetics is the handmaiden to evangelism." Do you see how good answers and evidence can address a person's spiritual sticking point, as it did for John, and open them up to the gospel message? Is there someone you know who just needs some good answers and evidence? What can you do about that this week?

In the story, Mark had on hand a good book he could loan to John that would help answer John's questions and objections. Are there some good books you should keep handy to give to people in your life who have questions? If not, what's stopping you from picking up a few tools that might impact your friend's life and eternity?

Mark said he surprised even himself when he laid out the one-month spiritual goal to John. Do you think it might help some of your friends to issue a similar challenge? If so, who are you going to reach out to—and when?

Notes

1. Dr. Alexander Metherell, quoted in Lee Strobel, *The Case for Christ: A Journalist's Personal Investigation of the Evidence for Jesus* (Grand Rapids, Mich.: Zondervan, 1998), pp. 193–202.

2. William D. Edwards, et al., "On the Physical Death of Jesus Christ," *Journal of the American Medical Association* (March 21, 1986), pp. 1455–1463.

3. Gerd Lüdemann, *The Resurrection of Christ: A Historical Inquiry* (Amherst, N.Y.: Prometheus Books, 2004), p. 50.

4. James D. G. Dunn, *Jesus Remembered: Christianity in the Making* (Grand Rapids, Mich.: Eerdmans, 2003), p. 855, emphasis in original.

5. Bart D. Ehrman, *How Jesus Became God: The Exaltation of a Jewish Preachers from Galilee* (San Francisco: HarperOne, 2015).

6. Craig Evans, *How God Became Jesus: The Real Origins of Belief in Jesus' Divine Nature* (Grand Rapids, Mich.: Zondervan, 2014).

7. William Lane Craig, quoted in Lee Strobel, *The Case for Christ: A Journalist's Personal Investigation of the Evidence for Jesus*, pp. 239–240.

8. Evans, *How God Become Jesus.*

9. Michael Licona, cited in Lee Strobel, *In Defense of Jesus: Investigating Attacks on the Identity of Christ* (Grand Rapids, Mich.: Zondervan, 2016), p. 125.

10. Gerd Lüdemann, *What Really Happened to Jesus: A Historical Approach to the Resurrection* (Louisville, Ky.: John Knox Press, 1995), p. 80.

SESSION FIVE

EXPLAINING THE CENTRAL MESSAGE OF CHRIST

But as many as received Him, to them He gave the right to become children of God, even to those who believe in His name.

JOHN 1:12 NASB

Getting Started

Welcome back for session five of *Making Your Case for Christ*. Today we're going to focus on the core message of the Christian faith—the gospel—and how we can make it clear for our friends. But first, let's pause to see who was able to get into conversations this past week about what we discussed in the last session concerning the evidence for Jesus' resurrection. How did it go?

Quick quiz time: Who would like to remind the group of what the Four *E*'s of the resurrection stand for? Remember, this is life-giving information for people who don't yet know Christ, just as it was for Lee Strobel during his search for truth. Also, let's keep praying and looking for open doors to discuss these matters with the people around us. They're more interested than we think they are—and they really do need what we have to share!

Opening Discussion

As we saw in session one, a foundational verse for this course is 1 Peter 3:15. It's in that verse that Peter tells us to be prepared to give an answer to everyone who asks us about our faith. In a similar vein, Paul challenges us in Colossians 4:5 to "be wise in the way you act toward outsiders; make the most of every opportunity."

- What do you think Paul was getting at when he told us to "make the most of every opportunity"? Can you think of any upcoming opportunities you should get ready for?

- Have you ever had a chance to talk about your faith but wished you had been more prepared for it? What happened?

- Suppose a newer acquaintance came up to you this week and said, "I know you go to church and seem pretty serious about spiritual stuff. Can you explain to me what your faith is all about?" Do you know what you would say?

This is what today's session is all about—helping us make sure we're ready to explain the central Christian message in a way that will be clear and helpful to our friends. While we're not going to learn some drawn-out memorized speech, it will be helpful for us to have a simple illustration ready to allow us to do what the verse in Colossians tells us to do—"make the most of every opportunity" to share our faith with others.

So, let's get started with this week's teaching.

"For I am not ashamed of the gospel, because it is the power of God that brings salvation to everyone who believes: first to the Jew, then to the Gentile." — Romans 1:16

Video Teaching

Watch the video for session five, in which Lee and Mark discuss the topic of this session: "Explaining the Central Message of Christ." As you watch, use the following outline to record any thoughts or concepts that stand out to you.

Opening Vignette

Our privilege today is that we get to tell people about the gospel message, and help them take the first step toward putting their trust in Jesus. There's nothing like being a witness to God transforming another person's heart and life.

Opening Teaching

It's not enough to just have head knowledge about Christ—to nod our heads and say, "Yes, I agree with what the Bible says." We need to take the next step to actually *respond*.

Movie Clip

In the clip, watch how Lee explains to Leslie that the weight of the evidence for the Christian faith has led him to a decision—and how Leslie then guides him in how to *respond* to that realization by leading him in a prayer to accept Jesus as his Forgiver and Leader.

Main Teaching

We're ultimately trying to help our friends and family members reach the point where they humble themselves before God, put their trust in him, and experience salvation in Christ.

John 1:12 provides us with the elements of a "faith formula" we can use to help our friends and family members make a decision to follow Christ:

B _____. *What information do I need to accept? Does it make sense? Are there good reasons for me to trust this information?*

R _____. *What do I need to do with what I've learned? What do I need to acknowledge about myself? What do I want to ask Christ to do for me?*

B _____. *Where does following these first two steps lead me? What change does this bring in my standing before God?*

The adventure of the Christian life really begins when we go through the steps of *Believe + Receive = Become.* Our former selves are gone, and our new life in Christ begins (2 Corinthians 5:17).

We can use these elements in John 1:12 as a diagnostic tool to help us understand at which stage in the process our friends or family members may be spiritually stuck.

Video Wrap

The *Believe + Receive = Become* framework can help us meet our friends where they are, and it can enable us to understand the obstacles they need to overcome in their journey toward becoming a child of God.

> *"Therefore, if anyone is in Christ, the new creation has come: The old has gone, the new is here!"* — 2 Corinthians 5:17

Group Interaction

The faith formula gives you a simple outline to help you not only present the message of the gospel but also to diagnose where your friends are spiritually and what you can do to help them in their journeys toward faith. For example, are they still on their way to the *Believe* stage, like Lee was during most of *The Case for Christ* movie? If so, they may need you to provide them with more information and evidence (see the resources listed on the Further Reading page in the back of this study guide for some ideas).

Or maybe your friends are already at *Believe*, but they need your help in how to respond to what they now know about Christ—how to make the Savior of the world *their* Savior. Now you know how to help them get beyond merely agreeing and acknowledging that it is intellectually true, to the point where they *Receive* Jesus' forgiveness and leadership for their lives from this point forward. Remember that an example such as Mark's aviation illustration from the teaching can help them to see that they need to get beyond just nodding their head in agreement—they need to climb on board with Christ!

And, in some cases, we'll talk to people who really do *Believe* and understand they need to *Receive*, but who just haven't taken that step yet. They might need you to help them crystalize their situation a bit—and perhaps to give them a little nudge to climb on board before the plane leaves the gate and thus *Become* a child of God. We'll discuss how we can do that during our final session in this study.

- Thinking back on your own journey, can you see where in your life you went into the *Believe* stage, and then later to the *Receive* stage? It might have been so early in your experience that the two seem to be blended together, but for many Christians these stages are quite distinct. Do you have any examples?

- In diagnosing where your friends are in their faith journey, can you think of people you know who are still working toward the place where they can *Believe*? If so, they primarily need good information (and perhaps motivation to access the information available to them). Can you share about someone you're trying to reach in this situation? What do you think you might do to help him or her take the next step?

- Can you give an example of someone you're talking to who really does share your biblical beliefs but doesn't seem to be able to get to the point where they actually *Receive* Christ? What do you think you could do or say to get them moving forward? Does anyone else have any wisdom or suggestions to add for this situation?

 # Group Reflection

Take a few minutes now to review the faith formula, which is summarized below, and mark some key words or concepts to remember. Then pair up with someone you haven't practiced with yet to explain the *Believe + Receive = Become* message to each other. (Take a few minutes to review now, then take the time you need to practice talking it through with your partner, and then reverse roles and let them share it with you.)

Believe

In the movie clip, Lee realized what we need to help our friends discover: that it's not enough to "just have faith" without understanding what that faith is in. Put another way, Lee realized that faith is trust and trust is only as good as what you're trusting in. Is it really trustworthy? Does it have real facts and evidence backing it up?

This is why Lee researched the Christian faith so carefully. He knew Leslie's beliefs were sincere, but he feared they were sincerely wrong. Then, over time, he found the facts he needed, and they pointed to several essential truths of the Christian worldview. These are summed up in Romans 10:9–10:

> If you declare with your mouth, "Jesus is Lord," and believe in your heart that God raised him from the dead, you will be saved. For it is with your heart that you believe and are justified, and it is with your mouth that you profess your faith and are saved.

There are three nonnegotiable truths in this passage that a person must believe in order to receive salvation. First, that "Jesus is Lord"—which points to his divine nature as the Son of God. Second, that Jesus died for our sins (this is assumed in the next point). And third, that "God raised him from the dead." According to this passage, we must genuinely embrace these three truths in order to receive salvation.

Believe + Receive

The problem is that it's not enough to just accept these truths intellectually. The sobering reality is that many people—including those in churches—merely nod their heads in agreement with these facts but fail to respond appropriately to what they know.

Going back to the faith formula, it's not enough to just *velieve* the right things about God; we must also *receive* him in a personal way. How? By asking him to apply the important truths discussed above to our own lives. Specifically:

- By receiving Jesus, the eternal Son of God, as *our* God.
- By receiving Jesus' death on the cross as the payment for our sins— thus making him *our* Savior.
- By receiving the risen Jesus as *our* Leader.

To *receive* is to say yes to all we know to be true about Jesus, just as Lee did in the movie clip we watched during this session. It's putting our trust in him and cooperating with all he wants to do in and for us. And when we do this, we have completed the faith formula.

Believe + Receive = Become

When we *believe* the truth about Jesus' identity and mission, and when we *receive* what he has done for us on a personal level, then we *become* his children through adoption into his family. This is explained in Romans 8:14–16:

For those who are led by the Spirit of God are the children of God. The Spirit you received does not make you slaves, so that you live in fear again; rather, the Spirit you received brought about your adoption to sonship. And by him we cry, "*Abba,* Father." The Spirit himself testifies with our spirit that we are God's children.

This is an incredible truth. God could have just forgiven our sins and left us as mere servants in his kingdom—and we would have had much to thank him for. But he didn't stop with forgiveness. He went all the way to *adopting* us as his beloved sons and daughters; forgiven of our sins, yes, but also embraced as family members. This, truly, is *amazing grace!*

After practicing the faith formula with one other person, discuss the following questions:

- How did it go? Did you think your points were pretty clear? Did *the other person* think they were clear as well?

- Is there anything that you would do differently next time? What would it be?

- Who could you share this information with this week? If possible, explain it to someone who doesn't yet know Christ!

 # Conclusion

God can use each of us to share his good news with our family and friends. More than that, he wants to use us to lead them to faith in Christ—like we saw Leslie do with Lee in the movie. This is something *we* can do. God wants to use us to impact the lives and eternities of others. And as he reminded us in the Great Commission in Matthew 28:18–20, he will be with us as we go—always!

"Go and make disciples. . . . And surely I am with you always, to the very end of the age." — Matthew 28:19–20

Closing Challenge

In Romans 1:16, Paul tells us that the gospel message—the message we've been working to learn and communicate today—is "the power of God that brings salvation to everyone who believes: first to the Jew, then to the Gentile." This means two things: this message has incredible potency, and it's available for everyone!

We just need to take small risks to bring it up and explain to others how they can come to *believe* the right things about God, *receive* the forgiveness and leadership of Christ, and in the process to *become* dearly beloved children of God. Remember: we have great news to share—now we just need to spread it around!

So take some risks this week. Then, the next time we're together, you can share your stories about how God worked through you!

Finishing the Session

Let's close in prayer, thanking God that he has done everything necessary for our salvation—and for the salvation of our loved ones—and that all we need to do is embrace him and his provision for us. This really is amazingly good news. We can worship him for that, and ask him to turn us all into increasingly clear and courageous communicators of his gospel who will be used by him to bring many others into his ever-expanding family!

BETWEEN-SESSIONS
PERSONAL STUDY

Reflect on the content we've covered this week in *Making Your Case for Christ* by delving into any or all of the following *between-sessions* activities. As you do, let God encourage you through his Word and the information that follows. At your next meeting, there will be time for you to share with your group any key points or insights that stood out to you.

📖 Study God's Word

In the following section, we'll examine a series of key Bible verses along with reflection questions related to the things people need to *believe* in regard to the central message of Christ.

Jesus Was God in Human Flesh

In John 1:1–3 we read, "In the beginning was the Word, and the Word was with God, and the Word was God. He was with God in the beginning. Through him all things were made; without him nothing was made that has been made." In verse 14, we see that this is referring to Jesus, who "became flesh and made his dwelling among us." How does the biblical doctrine of the Trinity help us understand that Jesus "was with God," and that Jesus also "was God" (verse 1)?

In John 5:17, Jesus says, "My Father is always at his work to this very day, and I too am working." In the following verse, John explains that "For this reason they tried all the more to kill him; not only was he breaking the Sabbath, but he was even calling God his own Father, making himself equal with God" (verse 18). Some have tried to claim that Jesus, by calling himself "the Son of God," was saying he was *not* divine. But what does this passage tell you?

In John 10:30, Jesus said, "I and the Father are one." John goes on to tell us in verses 31–33, "Again his Jewish opponents picked up stones to stone him, but Jesus said to them, 'I have shown you many good works from the Father. For which of these do you stone me?' 'We are not stoning you for any good work,' they replied, 'but for blasphemy, because you, a mere man, claim to be God.'" This was a consistent charge from the religious leaders against Jesus. If Jesus were not claiming divinity, wouldn't he have pointed out they were misunderstanding him? Does he ever do so? What does this tell you about his identity?

Jesus Came to Die for Our Sins

Some 700 years before the time of Christ, Isaiah prophesied about one who would be "pierced for our transgressions [and] crushed for our iniquities." Isaiah also tells us, "The punishment that brought us peace was on him, and by his wounds we are healed" (Isaiah 53:5). Who does this sound like to you? Is there anyone *other than* Jesus who you think fits that description?

When John the Baptist announced Jesus' arrival, he referred to him as "the Lamb of God, who takes away the sin of the world" (John 1:29). What Old Testament practice was he referencing (see Exodus 29:38–42)? If Jesus "takes away the sin of the world," are any other sacrifices needed to pay for our salvation? Why or why not?

Jesus said he came "to give his life as a ransom for many" (Matthew 20:28). Jesus' sacrificial death paid the penalty we owed for our sins so that he could freely offer us his salvation. If Jesus was willing to go to such lengths to reach us, what does that inspire you to do in order to reach others?

Jesus Proved His Identity and Purpose by Rising from the Dead

Jesus staked all his claims on the fact that after he was put to death, he would rise again three days later. We studied this in session four when we discussed the "sign of Jonah." In several other places Jesus predicted these events, including Mark 8:31, where he said he must "suffer many things and be rejected by the elders, the chief priests and the teachers of the law, and that he must be killed and after three days rise again." Then, of course, he fulfilled these promises by rising from the dead on that first Easter morning. Jesus knew he would suffer an unjust death at the hands of the enemy. So why do you think he was willing to come at all?

Can you imagine trying to argue with someone who says, "I know I've made some big claims, but I'm going to prove they're all true by dying and then rising from the dead three days later"—*and then does it* (see John 2:18–22)? What might you say to your friends who are trying to argue with Jesus right now?

Based on the above information, Jesus was God in human flesh, he came to die for our sins, and he proved these things were true by rising from the dead. What would you like to say or offer to him as your response?

Put It into Practice

In the teaching for this session, Mark Mittelberg used an aviation illustration that can help your friends understand the gospel message, and especially the faith formula: *Believe + Receive = Become*. Here it is again for you to review and use with the people you talk to:

> Let's say a family member offers to fly you home for the holidays. It's a great offer, but getting home will require two things. First, you have to *believe* that airplanes fly. You'll never be willing to get on an airplane if you don't believe it will really get you over the mountains, right?
>
> But just believing that airplanes fly won't get you home either. You can be fully confident in the science of flight, even hang around an airport watching airplanes take off and land. But it takes more than belief in aviation to get home. You must also *receive* the ticket that was purchased for you and use it to board the airplane that is heading to your hometown. It's that combination of believing and receiving that allows you to *become* a passenger of that flight who will, as a result, get back home.

It is much the same with Christ. We need to go beyond merely *believing* that Jesus is the Son of God who died on the cross for our sins and who rose to give us life. We must take the next step and trust in him personally, *receiving* him as the forgiver of our sins and the leader of our life. That is the equivalent of "climbing on board" with Jesus in a way that will ultimately get us home spiritually, where we *become* his forgiven sons and daughters.

Is there someone you've been talking to about the gospel who would be helped by this illustration? Might God be prompting you to share it with that person, whether verbally, or by letter or email? If so, take the risk and see how he uses it!

 ## Reflect on a Key Story

The following is an encouraging account that Mark relates in *The Unexpected Adventure* about a man who didn't yet understand the life-changing message of the gospel. Take a moment to read it, and then consider your responses to the questions at the end.

The Power of the Gospel

Mark Mittelberg

I had been teaching a group of church leaders from all over the country and around the world for a couple of hours before we took a mid-morning break. My topic was how pastors and leaders could help church members clarify their own spiritual stories, including how they made their commitments to Christ and the difference that has produced in their lives.

We had enjoyed great interactions, including a lively time of questions and answers, and then during the break I chatted with people who wanted to discuss things further. As we were nearing the time when we needed to start the workshop again, a man who had been waiting stepped up to say something to me.

"I'm a bit troubled by something you've been talking about," Steve began, "and I wondered if you could help me sort it out."

"I'd be happy to try," I said. "What's your concern?"

"Well," he replied, "you've been describing the Christian life with phrases like 'becoming a believer' and 'the point when a person trusts in Christ.' But some of us come from faith traditions that don't really talk that way. We don't emphasize conversion experiences or spiritual crisis points in a person's life. We tend to talk more about simply growing up in the faith, believing in God, participating in the church, and so forth. So given our emphasis, how would you apply what you've been teaching this morning to our situation?"

"That's a great question," I began, "because I know there really is a difference in how various groups of Christians describe what needs to happen in a person's life. Some parts of the church world emphasize the importance of a person having a dramatic moment of turning from sin to follow Christ. Others stress the need for people to understand this increasingly over time, leading them to embrace Christ during the process of learning about the truths of Christianity. And if that can happen naturally as a child grows up, it can lead to a consistent and stable faith."

Steve nodded affirmingly.

"But I do need to caution," I added, "that it's not always just a matter of semantics or emphasis. Sometimes I think people feel uncomfortable with talking about conversion or 'making a commitment to Christ' because in reality they've never actually taken that step themselves. In fact, I think there are a lot of people in churches who have just jumped on a bandwagon, which is easy to do these days when so many churches have such great bands. But they've never really internalized the message and asked Jesus to become their own forgiver and leader—"

Steve suddenly *burst into tears*. He was fairly discreet about it, but he didn't try to hide that I had hit a nerve. As he regained his composure, he attempted to explain why he thought my words had touched him at such a deep level. I encouraged him and listened as he spoke.

I soon realized, however, that we were a couple of minutes past the allotted time for the break and that most of the group were already back in the room, getting ready for me to start teaching again.

So I said, "Steve, this is obviously a very important discussion, and I don't want to shortchange it by trying to finish it quickly right this moment. Immediately after this next session, we're going to take a longer lunch break. Can we get together then and keep talking?"

Steve agreed. As soon as our group broke for lunch, he and I dashed to my car to drive to a nearby sandwich shop. Knowing the time would go quickly, we jumped back into our discussion as we drove.

Steve described to me what he had been realizing all morning, which was what I'd suspected. He had been involved for years in a variety of church programs and activities, but he had never actually asked Jesus to be his Savior. Steve was religious, but he didn't have a real relationship with Christ. This had now become clear in his mind, and for obvious reasons it was very troubling to him.

As I parked the car next to a deli, I tried to impress upon him that many people are in this situation and that he didn't need to feel embarrassed. But I also urged him not to stay in that situation any longer. I told him I believed God had led him to our workshop to hear the truth, and that God was graciously opening Steve's eyes to his need to receive the salvation Jesus paid for by dying on the cross.

As I explained the gospel, Steve readily agreed with all that I said, and tears welled up in his eyes again as he affirmed that he wanted to know that he was forgiven for his sins and had become a true member of God's family.

"Steve," I said, "you can seal that decision right now by praying with me, right here, to receive God's gift of grace and leadership."

He was more than ready, so together—sitting in my car in the parking lot outside Schlotzsky's Deli—we prayed and Steve asked Jesus to be his Savior and Lord.

It was an amazing moment. You might wonder how to celebrate after something like this. We wondered the same thing, but while we were considering the question, we hurried in and had sandwiches.

As we drove back to the church, I prayed again out loud, asking God to give Steve the assurance that he was now God's son and that he would be filled with joy. He later told me that as I spoke he kept praying, "Yes, Lord Jesus." He said that "suddenly the word *Lord* took on a whole new meaning. It was as if the four letters of that word radiated with red and blue and gold colors. I kept saying, 'Lord Jesus'—just those two words over and over. I finally understood the word *Lord* and I laughed and cried."

This truly was a turning point in Steve's life. Over the years, Steve has grown immensely in his faith, written a couple of devotional books, and even served for a season as the pastor of a church. I only spent about an hour with him that day, but thankfully God gave me the clarity to challenge him with the incisive truths of the gospel. Then I got to watch as God did the rest.

Talk about *adventure*!

This story illustrates what Mark and Lee discussed during the teaching: a lot of people are religious but don't really know Jesus. Does this bring a particular person or situation to mind? What could you say to bring clarity about that person's need for a real relationship with Christ?

Sometimes when a friend is substituting religion for a genuine walk with Christ, we need to take a risk and address him or her in a bold and clear way. What might you do in a similar situation as the one described in the story?

Has someone ever had to challenge your thinking in order to help you reassess your own relationship with God? Have you ever needed to do so for somebody else? In either case, why do you think it was worth the risk?

Proverbs 27:6 tells us that "wounds from a friend can be trusted." How does this encourage you for when you are in situations similar to the story above?

SESSION SIX

ENCOURAGING FRIENDS TO FOLLOW CHRIST

*God was reconciling the world to himself in Christ, not counting
people's sins against them. And he has committed to us
the message of reconciliation. We are therefore Christ's ambassadors,
as though God were making his appeal through us.*

2 CORINTHIANS 5:19–20

Getting Started

Welcome back! Before we launch into session six, let's take a couple minutes to hear any stories from this last week. Did you get to share the faith formula with someone? Or any of the evidence we've been discussing for the biblical record about Christ or his resurrection? As those of you with stories already know, learning about these things is good, but it all really comes to life when you talk about it with a friend or family member!

> "The one who plants and the one who waters have one purpose, and they will each be rewarded according to their own labor. For we are co-workers in God's service." — 1 Corinthians 3:8–9

Opening Discussion

Something you may have noticed from the stories we've been sharing in our group, as well as from your other efforts to tell friends about your faith, is that people rarely change their thinking or spiritual perspectives quickly. Usually it's a longer *process*.

- Think about your own spiritual story. Probably for many of us, it was an up-and-down journey to finally come to faith in Christ—even if much of that was at an early age. Was that true for you?

- Yes, there are those exciting Saul-to-Paul Damascus Road conversions—and we love to hear about them. But how have you seen that these stories are usually the *exception*, not the norm?

- In what ways does it encourage you to realize it is usually a process for people to come to faith? Does that give you more hope for some of the seemingly hard-to-reach people in your life? Why or why not?

To learn more about how we can help foster people's spiritual journey toward Christ, let's take a look at our final video with Lee and Mark.

▶ Video Teaching

Watch the video for session six, in which the guys discuss the topic of this final session: "Encouraging Friends to Follow Christ." As you watch, use the following outline to record any ideas that stand out to you.

Opening Vignette

We need to remember that leading our friends and family members to Christ is a process that could take a long time. We have to be careful not to lose heart when we encounter setbacks, but persevere in praying for them and helping them get past their spiritual sticking points.

Opening Teaching

We want to help our loved ones make a spiritual *discovery* that leads to a *decision* to follow Christ that ultimately leads to making a *difference* in their lives, both now and for all of eternity.

Movie Clip

In the clip, notice how "Kenny London," the religious editor at the newspaper, prodded Lee to make a decision based on where the evidence for Christ seemed to be leading him.

Main Teaching

There are at least eight things we can do to actively participate in the work the Holy Spirit is doing in the lives of our friends and family members:

Real **R**_____—we need to get out of the mentality that the people we're trying to reach are "projects."

Honest **C**_____—we need to get real with our loved ones, and initiate appropriate spiritual interactions with them.

Faithful **P**_____—we need to remember that people come to Christ because *God* is at work in their lives, and faithfully do our part to help foster his activity.

P _____ and **P**_____—we need to seek God's wisdom to know when to give our friends room to process what they're learning versus trying to prod them forward.

I _____ and **E**_____—we have to remember that people have spiritual doubts and be prepared to give answers.

Central **M**_____ of the **G**_____—we must explain to our friends and family members the good news to which the evidence ultimately points.

Friendly **N**_____—sometimes we need to be direct and challenge our loved ones to act on what they're learning about Christ.

Spiritual **O**_____—we need to open the door at some point and tell our friends and family members that they can respond to God's offer of salvation—even at that very moment!

Video Wrap

In the Great Commission, Jesus told us to go into all the world, teach the truth, and present the message of the gospel. But he also reminded us that he would always be with us, helping us as we make our case for him (see Matthew 28:18–20).

Jesus also said we are the salt of the earth and the light of the world (see Matthew 5:13–14). He wants us to live in such a way that we make people thirst for God and sense the light of God's hope in the dark areas of despair.

Group Interaction

The teaching for this session gave a good summary of a number of elements for us to keep in mind as we seek to reach our friends and family members for Christ. Let's discuss a few of those elements together as a group.

- Do you have any quick thoughts or reactions to what we just heard?

- Were there any elements that surprised you—or any other elements that you thought should have been mentioned?

- We've covered a lot of ground in this session—and in the five sessions before it. Are you growing in your sense of confidence that you can effectively share your faith with others? Is there anything else you need in order to feel more confident?

Let's continue by taking a few minutes to review these eight elements, as summarized below. Write down any thoughts you want to remember under each of them. Then we'll have some further discussion together about these important themes.

1. Real Relationship

We saw this in the movie clip in Kenny London's friendship with Lee Strobel—and also between Lee and Leslie. Why is this so important? Because friends listen to friends. If we want to influence the people around us, we need to get close enough for them to want to open up to us. To confide in us. To share their spiritual questions and concerns.

Jesus was called "the friend of sinners" (Luke 7:34). And he was sometimes accused of committing the sins his non-believing friends were known for. But that was a misunderstanding he was willing to deal with in his efforts "to seek and to save the lost" (19:10). We need to imitate him and, with his help, to reach our friends with his message.

"John the Baptist came neither eating bread nor drinking wine, and you say, 'He has a demon.' The Son of Man came eating and drinking, and you say, 'Here is a glutton and a drunkard, a friend of tax collectors and sinners.' " — Luke 7:33–34

2. Honest Conversation

The person you hope to reach may be a family member or a friend who you've known for a long time. But that doesn't necessarily mean you have the kind of trusting relationship that will be conducive for honest conversations about personal beliefs, questions, and struggles. Sometimes we need to first take deliberate steps to deepen the friendship. This usually involves finding safe places where we can talk openly, and it often requires us first being vulnerable about our own journey, including setbacks and struggles we've faced along the way. Also, this is not something you can rush. Real relationships require plenty of hangout time.

There's a scene in the movie where Alfie and Leslie are talking in the park about what Leslie can do to better reach out to Lee. Alfie asked Leslie how she used to reach him, and she replied, "We'd talk—really talk—and *listen*." Alfie responded, "Listen? *Do that*!"

This is the most overlooked part of relationships and conversations. Our tendency is to fill in all the spaces by talking on and on. But instead we need to do what Jesus did: ask questions and wait for a response. Draw the other person out. Really listen, and then respond to their thoughts, concerns, and questions. In so doing they'll feel understood—and loved. And that will help them trust you and want to open up to you even more.

3. Faithful Prayer

This is easy to neglect, but we must lift our friend up to God in prayer, asking that he will use us, give us the right words and demeanor, and by his Holy Spirit draw that person to Christ. We need to remind ourselves that nothing will really happen unless *God* is at work. Prayer is how we invite God's activity.

In the movie, we saw Leslie praying a prayer that she learned from Scripture and from Alfie. It's in Ezekiel 36:26, and it says this: "I will give you a new heart and put a new spirit within you; and I will remove the heart of stone . . . and give you a heart of flesh" (NASB). Leslie prayed that verse—and claimed that verse for Lee—for nearly two years. God heard and honored her prayer. He'll honor your prayers too, but you need to pray faithfully.

4. Patience and Persistence

As we've explained in the other sessions, coming to Christ is almost always a process. So we need to cooperate with God in that process. This is another reason we need to keep praying, asking God for wisdom along the way.

The movie portrays well what was true in real life. Leslie was exceedingly patient as Lee went through all kinds of spiritual ups and downs. He'd get angry and pull back. Then he'd show a glimmer of interest and her hope would grow— only to be dashed again. We need God's grace to show *patience* through a process like that.

But we also need courage to be appropriately *persistent*, like Leslie was when she brought Lee coffee and challenged him to come to church with her and the kids. God used that tenacious side of her, too. We all need a mix of patience and persistence—and God's wisdom to know which of these to lean toward when.

5. Information and Evidence

People's resistance to God is often due to a lack of understanding of him and what he wants of us. Lee was surprised when he first visited the church with Leslie and understood the message of grace. He had always thought the Christian faith was based on being a good person, and trying to follow the rules. He needed better information.

But Lee also needed evidence that proved the information was true. Could the Bible be trusted? Did Jesus back up his claim to be the Son of God? Did he really rise from the dead? This evidence was vital for Lee to keep moving forward spiritually.

That means we need to do our homework so we'll be able to help dispense the needed information. We need to keep on reading, studying, and looking up answers to tough questions. We should be ready to give people good books, or to invite them to church services or to our class or small group, where they can ask their questions and get real answers.

What if we don't know the answers to the questions they're asking? That's okay—just admit it, and then do a little research so you can get back with them with an answer a few days later. God will deepen you along the way, and your friend will appreciate your efforts and input.

6. Central Message of the Gospel

More than just general biblical information, our friends need to understand the central message of the Christian faith, the gospel. In many ways, everything else leads to this message—that we're sinners in need of a Savior. He is one who, thankfully, came to bring us salvation. He paid the penalty for our sins. He loves us. He wants to forgive us and set us on a new direction, to adopt us into his family, and to lead our lives.

How should we respond to that message? Maybe this will sound familiar, but we need to *Believe* the truth about who Jesus is and what he offers us, and then to turn from our sins and humbly pray to *Receive* his forgiveness and leadership in our lives. When we've done this, we can be confident that we've been adopted into his family and have literally *Become* a child of God.

In Romans 1:16, Paul tells us the gospel is the "power of God that brings salvation to everyone who believes." So share it with the boldness that comes from knowing you are wielding the message that is literally "the power of God" for the salvation of your friends.

"More than just general biblical information, our friends need to understand the central message of the Christian faith, the gospel. In many ways, everything else leads to this message— that we're sinners in need of a Savior."

7. Friendly Nudges

The scene we watched during the teaching shows Kenny London, who had been pretty mild-mannered throughout the movie, finally getting fed up and challenging Lee to "put up or shut up" and to "stop blaming me, and the church, and God." He tells Lee, "Do your job. Stack up the evidence, follow the facts, and write the story—win or lose!" It was the kind of spiritual jolt Lee needed. Most of us have likely needed something similar along the way.

It may feel intimidating to challenge your friend. You will need to do so in a way that fits your personality and the relationship you have with that person, and in a spirit that shows you are motivated by love. You'll need wisdom from the Holy Spirit concerning how and when to give that person a nudge. And you may need to do so more than once. But be willing to give that gentle push, because that's what it takes for many people to get off of dead center and to take that vital step of faith into God's family.

8. Spiritual Opportunity

Finally, we need to be ready and willing to open the door for our friend to actually pray to receive Christ. We saw this in the movie clip last week when Leslie told Lee he could receive Christ right there on the spot. Do you remember what he said? *"Now?"* he asked. "Don't we have to go to church?" Leslie replied, "Nope, right here, right now—this is church!" She then briefly explained the faith formula and led him to pray, in his own words, acknowledging his need for Christ—and God did the rest!

We need to be willing to take a small risk to find out if our friends are ready. We need to be sure we're ready as well. Here's a tip that might help: when you pray with your friends to receive Christ, use the faith formula as an outline for the prayer! Specifically, have your friends talk to God, out loud, and do the following:

- Acknowledge that they *Believe* they are sinners in need of the Savior, that forgiveness is available through Jesus' death, and that new life is available because he rose from the dead and is there to help.

- Express that they want to turn from their sins and *Receive* Jesus as their Savior and Lord. Or, as Lee and Mark often describe it, as their Forgiver and Leader.

- After addressing the *Believe* and *Receive* parts, have them thank God that they've now *Become* his child—right then and there. This helps them trust that he has already heard and responded to their prayer, just as he promised he would (see 1 John 1:9).

Group Reflection

Now that we've taken the time to reflect on each of these elements and write down a few notes, let's break into groups of four to six people to discuss the following:

- Which of these eight elements were the most important in the process of your own journey toward faith in Christ?

- Which of these do you feel your family members or friends most need from you right now?

- Is there something else that wasn't mentioned that you think your friends need most?

- Is there one or more of these broad areas that you sense you need to focus on more in your efforts to reach others? Which areas?

- Would anyone share any specific steps you sense God leading you to take to grow in this area—or maybe a risk you think he is asking you to take to better reach out to your friend?

Before we end, let's take a few minutes to pair up one more time to pray for each other as we continue to reach out to our family and friends to *make our case for Christ.*

 ## Conclusion

Here is a closing reminder of what we've covered during these six sessions—areas in which we're now more ready to let God use us as we reach out to our friends for him.

In session one, we learned about the importance of *helping our friends consider the case for Christ.* We hope you now see that nothing could be more important than this!

In session two, we learned *how we can describe our own spiritual journey with Christ*. We talked about how we can share, in three parts, what spiritual truths we came to *discover*, what that led us to *decide*, and how that decision has made a *difference* in our lives.

In session three, we talked about how we can *back up the biblical record of Christ* using the A-E-I-O-U acronym. We learned that the Gospels exhibit clear *Authorship*; they're *Early Writings*; there is *Integrity of the Text*, we have *Outside Corroboration*, and they exhibit *Uniqueness*.

In session four, we discovered how we can *present evidence for the resurrection of Christ* using the Four E's: *Execution, Early Accounts, Empty Tomb*, and *Eyewitnesses*.

In session five, we learned—and practiced—*how to explain the central message of Christ, the gospel*. We used the faith formula: *Believe + Receive = Become*, which we should all by now have down cold!

And now, in session six, we have discussed eight key elements that will help us better *encourage our friends to follow Christ*.

Closing Challenge

Don't forget what Lee and Mark said at the end of today's teaching: *You can do this!* God has called you to share his truth with clarity and confidence but also with gentleness and respect. He wants to use each of us to reach our friends for him.

"Moreover, I will give you a new heart and put a new spirit within you; and I will remove the heart of stone from your flesh and give you a heart of flesh. I will put My Spirit within you and cause you to walk in My statutes." — *Ezekiel 36:26–27* NASB

Finishing the Session

Let's close in prayer, asking God to help us remember what we've learned during these six sessions, to have the courage to put this information into action, and to have his power working through us so that our friends and family members will find our case for Christ compelling, leading many of them to receive his forgiveness and grace.

BETWEEN-SESSIONS
PERSONAL STUDY

Reflect on the content we covered in our final session of *Making Your Case for Christ* by engaging in the following personal study activities. This will help seal your understanding of the eight elements we discussed related to how we can encourage our friends to follow Christ.

📖 Study God's Word

In the following section, we'll examine eight Bible passages that underscore the importance of each of the elements we discussed during this session, followed by a reflection question to help you apply it in your own life.

Real Relationship

Read Luke 19:1–10 to see how Jesus reached out to Zacchaeus, the tax collector (maybe you remember the children's song, "a wee little man was he!"), who had climbed a sycamore tree in the effort to get a better glimpse of the famed teacher. What do Jesus' actions tell you about the need for—as well as the potential in—building *real relationships* with people who are far from God?

Honest Conversation

Read John 4:1–42 to see how Jesus sought out the Samaritan woman and engaged her in an *honest conversation* about her relationship with the Father. Notice how he initiated their discussion, turned ordinary topics into spiritual interactions, side-stepped superfluous questions to focus on substantial subjects, and got personal with her about her need for a Savior. How does his example inspire or challenge you in your own conversations with friends who don't yet know God?

Faithful Prayer

In Ezekiel 36:26–27, God says, "I will give you a new heart and put a new spirit in you; I will remove from you your heart of stone and give you a heart of flesh. And I will put my Spirit in you and move you to follow my decrees." As you saw in the movie clip, this is the passage that inspired Leslie Strobel's *faithful prayer* for her then-skeptical husband. It didn't happen right away, but ultimately Lee's heart was changed and Leslie's prayer was answered. How does this inspire you to pray for the loved ones you hope to reach for Christ?

Patience and Persistence

In 2 Timothy 4:2, Paul admonishes, "Preach the word; be prepared in season and out of season; correct, rebuke and encourage—with great patience and careful instruction." What lessons can you draw out of this passage about your need for both *patience and persistence* in your evangelistic efforts?

Information and Evidence

In John 10:37–38, Jesus said to his critics, "Do not believe me unless I do the works of my Father. But if I do them, even though you do not believe me, believe the works, that you may know and understand that the Father is in me, and I in the Father." In other words, Jesus was saying that if his critics were unwilling to take him at his word, then they ought to look at the broader *information and evidence* that was seen through his works, including his divine insights and miraculous actions, and be convinced by those. So Jesus pointed to evidence, as did Paul and other writers of Scripture. How important is it for you, then, to know and use evidence in reaching people who are skeptical about the claims of Christianity? What further steps do you think would help you grow more confident in this area?

Central Message of the Gospel

The apostle Paul was highly educated and could teach about many important topics—and often did. Yet in 1 Corinthians 2:2, he said, "For I resolved to know nothing while I was with you except Jesus Christ and him crucified." In other words, he was making it clear that nothing would sidetrack him from focusing on the *central message of the gospel*—the good news of salvation that is available to us through Christ and his finished work on the cross. What lessons can you draw from this? Is there someone you've been talking to about a variety of spiritual topics, but he or she needs you to bring the conversation to a head by asking where he or she stands with Jesus and his offer of salvation?

Friendly Nudges

In Revelation 3:2–3, Jesus admonished, "Wake up! Strengthen what remains and is about to die, for I have found your deeds unfinished in the sight of my God. Remember, therefore, what you have received and heard; hold it fast, and repent. But if you do not wake up, I will come like a thief, and you will not know at what time I will come to you." Peter told us in 1 Peter 3:15 to treat people with "gentleness and respect"—but there are times when we must give *friendly nudges* to the people we're trying to reach. In fact, many of them won't move forward spiritually until we finally look them in the eye and tell them it's time to "Wake up!" Is there anyone in your life who needs that kind of jolt from you? What will you do?

Spiritual Opportunity

Jesus said, "Come to me, all you who are weary and burdened, and I will give you rest. Take my yoke upon you and learn from me, for I am gentle and humble in heart, and you will find rest for your souls. For my yoke is easy and my burden is light" (Matthew 11:28–30). And the last chapter in the Bible extends this gracious, open-ended invitation: "The Spirit and the bride say, 'Come!' And let the one who hears say, 'Come!' Let the one who is thirsty come; and let the one who wishes take the free gift of the water of life" (Revelation 22:17). God's salvation is available to everyone—including our family members and friends. Sometimes we just need to give them a *spiritual opportunity* to respond to God's invitation. What about in your life? Does anyone you know come to mind? Why not reach out to them today?

Put It into Practice

For this final "Put It into Practice" section, take some time to page back through the contents of this study guide to remind yourself of all you've learned, and then put it into action by sharing it with the people in your life who need to hear it most. Review. Pray. Shoot a text message or make the call. Get together and take a small risk and share whatever God has been telling you to say. God will use you, some of your friends will find a faith like yours, and they'll thank you for all of eternity for *making your case for Christ*!

Reflect on a Key Story

In this final account from *The Unexpected Adventure*, Lee Strobel tells about his efforts to share Christ with an old friend from college. Read it and be encouraged, and then reflect on the four questions listed after the story.

Hang Time

Lee Strobel

I pulled up to my friend's house in a tiny convertible sports car. "You want us to drive across the country in *that*?" he said with a laugh.

"What do you mean?" I replied, feigning indignation. "Leslie and I drove all the way from Illinois to Florida in it last year."

He looked incredulous. "On *purpose*?"

Soon we were bantering like old times. Tarik and I had met as students at the University of Missouri, and on weekends we hitchhiked across the prairie to check out custom motorcycle shops in Joplin and Kansas City. Our wanderlust continued after we graduated, including a trip down to New Orleans during the Super Bowl to explore Bourbon Street and the rowdy football parties going on before and after the event. But now we were about to embark on an adventure with more serious overtones.

Because Tarik was working in Iowa and I lived in Chicago, we hadn't seen each other for several years. However, I heard vague rumors that he was facing some personal opportunities and challenges, and I doubted whether he had anyone he could trust to talk to about them. Besides, we had never really discussed my newfound faith in Christ.

So I called and said, "Hey, remember those road trips we used to go on? Let's take a week off from work and drive."

Surprisingly, Tarik didn't need any convincing. "All right. Why not? Pick me up."

He didn't ask what I would be driving, hence his dismay when I showed up in a blue Mazda Miata with the top down. The car barely seats two, but he squeezed inside and off we headed west without any particular destination in mind.

I don't think we turned on the radio the whole way. We just talked and talked. Actually, my role for the first couple of days was simply to listen. He was troubled about some impending decisions, and so for hours on end he discussed them in depth. I offered advice whenever I could.

Before long, we hit Omaha, had a nice steak dinner, and then decided to turn south. In Kansas, driving down U.S. Highway 281, we stumbled upon the geographical center of the forty-eight states, marked by a small monument and a tiny chapel that might seat six people. We ventured inside, where I pretended to preach a sermon; Tarik, raised in a Muslim home, didn't look very comfortable in the wooden pew.

Soon after that we were zipping down Highway 24 through Cawker City, Kansas, when I slammed on the brakes, put the car in reverse, and backed up to confirm what I thought I had seen. Sure enough, it was the World's Biggest Ball of Twine, all seven million feet of it, coiled into a ball approaching ten feet in diameter and enshrined in a large gazebo. Not quite awe-inspiring, but certainly worth a couple of campy photos.

As we approached Kansas City, our conversation turned to faith. The thorny challenges he was facing, I said to Tarik, might be less daunting if he had the comfort, wisdom, and guidance of Christ in his life.

Having been born in an Islamic country, Tarik was culturally Muslim, but he wasn't actively devout. When we were in college, the topic of religion came up only once, when we got into a disagreement about God. Tarik was aghast that I *didn't* believe in him, while I was astounded that he *did*.

As we drove, I told him the story of how I investigated the evidence for Jesus, and I described the way my new faith had changed my worldview, attitudes, and priorities. We stopped in Kansas City and went to a Royals baseball game that night, chattering about Christianity between innings. The following day we headed down Interstate 70 to Columbia to visit the University of Missouri, where we had met more than twenty years earlier.

We had a great time exploring our old dormitory and hangouts. At the end of the day, I stopped at a Christian bookstore so I could buy a Bible for Tarik. The next morning, before we left the hotel, I said to him, "Let me clarify what

Christianity is about." I leafed through the New Testament to Romans 6:23: "For the wages of sin is death, but the gift of God is eternal life in Christ Jesus our Lord."

"That," I said to Tarik, "pretty much sums it up. We deserve death, eternal separation from God, because of our sin or wrong-doing. But God offers us forgiveness and eternal life as a gift, purchased when Jesus died on the cross as our substitute to pay for all of our transgressions." I emphasized the word *gift* to contrast with Muslim teachings, which emphasize doing good works to try to appease Allah.

Tarik listened politely but didn't say much about this. As we headed north toward Iowa, I would bring up the gospel from time to time, but he seemed reluctant to talk about it. I tried not to get discouraged, telling myself that he was probably mulling over the implications of the verse. But deep inside I wondered. His personal challenges were weighing heavily on him. Did he see Jesus as a potential help or as a meaningless diversion?

It was late when we returned to his house. "I've got to leave early in the morning," I said as I was getting ready to head to the guest room. I was going to leave it at that, but I decided to take one more shot.

"Remember, we talked about how the Bible says forgiveness and eternal life are a gift," I said. "Would you like to pray with me to receive that gift? We could do that right here, right now."

His response stunned me. "Yes," he said. "I'd like to do that." And that evening, Tarik prayed with me to make Christ his Savior.

I cranked up the praise music as I drove back to Chicago the following morning. Tarik and I had spent five days meandering around the countryside. We had given up precious vacation time from work in order to spend those days hanging out together. But it was, I mused, a small investment compared to the eternal results.

Sometimes we won't reach our friends for Christ until we're willing to take more radical measures to do so. Lee took almost a week to drive around the country with his old friend in order to tell him about his new faith. What radical step do you think God might be telling you to take (*besides* buying a convertible)?

It's always tempting to say *no* for our friends before we give them the chance to say *yes* to Christ. Given that Tarik had been raised in the Muslim faith, that's certainly something Lee might have been tempted to do. Thankfully, he wasn't! Is there someone you've been saying no for? Are you willing to give that person the chance to say yes? What is your next step to take in doing that?

Lee wrote, "I was going to leave it at that, but I decided to take one more shot." Just imagine if he had really *left it at that*. Is there someone with whom you need to "take one more shot"? When will you do so?

After praying with Tarik to receive Christ, Lee "cranked up the praise music" while driving back home. He was having a heavenly celebration—here on earth. We've tried to convey throughout this course that there is nothing more rewarding than impacting another person's life for all of eternity. Have you experienced that yet? Have you experienced it lately? Don't you want to experience it a lot more?

Take a few minutes to pray and ask God to give you the wisdom, the clarity, the courage, the opportunities, and whatever else you need to be able to—as Jesus put it in John 15:5—"bear much fruit."

LEADER'S GUIDE

Thank you for your willingness to lead a group through the *Making Your Case for Christ* training course! What you have chosen to do is important, and great impact can come through courses like this. The rewards of being a leader are different from those of participating, and we hope that as you lead you will find your own walk with God deepened by this experience.

Making Your Case for Christ is a six-session study built around video content and small-group interaction. As the group leader (or, as Lee and Mark will sometimes refer to you in the videos, as the group facilitator), imagine yourself as the host of a dinner party. Your role is to take care of your guests by managing all of the behind-the-scenes details so that as your guests arrive they can focus on one another and on interacting around the course topics.

As the group leader, your aim should not be to answer all of the questions or reteach the content—the video and this study guide will do most of that work. Your job is to guide the experience and cultivate your small group into being a learning community. This will make it a place for members to process, question, and reflect—not receive more instruction.

There are several elements in this leader's guide that will help you as you structure your study and reflection time, so follow along and take advantage of each one.

Before You Begin

Prior to your first meeting, make sure the group members have a copy of this study guide so they can follow along and write out their notes and answers to the questions as they go through the material. Alternately, you can hand out the study guides at your first meeting and give the members time to look over the materials and ask any questions they might have. During your first meeting, send a sheet around the room and have the members write down their name, phone number, and email address so you can keep in touch with them during the week.

Generally, the ideal size for a group is eight to ten people, which ensures everyone will have time to participate in discussions. It's great if you have more people than that, but we would suggest breaking up the main group into smaller subgroups during discussion times. Encourage those who show up at the first meeting to commit to attending the duration of the course, as this will help your members get to know one another, create stability for the group, and help you know how to prepare each week.

Each of the sessions begins with a brief introduction followed by some opening discussion questions to get the group members focused and thinking about the topic at hand. Some people may want to relate a long story or personal experience in response to one of these questions, but the goal is to keep the answers fairly brief. Ideally, you want everyone in the group to get a chance to answer, so try to keep the responses to a minute or less. If you have talkative members, explain up front that everyone needs to limit their answer to one minute.

Give the members a chance to answer these questions, but tell them to feel free to pass if they wish. With the rest of the study, it's generally not a good idea to have everyone answer every question—a free-flowing discussion is more desirable. But with the opening questions, you can go around the circle. Encourage shy people to share, but don't force them to do so.

At your first meeting, let the group members know that each session contains three *Between-Sessions* activities that they can complete during the week. While this is an optional exercise, it can help them cement the concepts presented during the group meeting, encourage them to spend time each day in God's Word, and give them practical tools they can put into action to help them with the weekly group challenge. Invite group members to bring any questions or insights they uncover to your next meeting, especially if they had a breakthrough moment or didn't understand something.

Weekly Preparation

As the leader, there are a few things you should do to prepare for each meeting:

- *Read through the session.* This will help you to become familiar with the content and know how to structure the discussion times.

- *Decide which questions you definitely want to discuss.* Based on the amount and length of group discussion, you may not be able to get through all of the material, so choose four to five questions that you want to be sure to cover.

- *Be familiar with the questions you want to discuss.* When the group meets, you will naturally be aware of the clock, so make sure you have thought through the questions you have selected. This will help you make the most of the discussion time.

- *Pray for your group.* Pray for each of your group members throughout the week, asking God to lead them as they study his Word and learn how to effectively make their case for Christ to their friends and family members who are in need of God's message of hope and grace.

- *Bring extra supplies to your meeting.* The members should bring their own pens for writing notes, but it's a good idea to have a few extras available for those who forget. You may also want to bring paper and additional Bibles.

Note, too, that in many cases there will be no one "right" answer to the question. Answers will vary, especially when the group members are being asked to share their personal experiences.

Structuring the Discussion Time

As the group leader, it is up to you to track the time and keep things moving along according to the schedule you set. You might want to set a timer for each segment so both you and the group members know when your time is up. (Note there are some good phone apps for timers that play a gentle chime or other pleasant sound instead of a disruptive noise.)

Don't be concerned if the group members are quiet or slow to share. People are often quiet when they are pulling together their ideas, and this might be a new experience for them. Just ask a question and let it hang in the air until someone speaks up. You can then say, "Thank you. What about others? What came to your mind when you heard this question?"

Keep in mind that, generally, most groups will be able to cover the content in this course in one hour to 90 minutes. So, you can use one of these schedules:

Section	60 Minutes	90 Minutes
OPENING DISCUSSION (discuss the opening questions for the session)	10 minutes	15 minutes
VIDEO (watch the teaching video together and write down some notes)	25 minutes	25 minutes
GROUP INTERACTION/REFLECTION (discuss the questions that you selected ahead of time)	20 minutes	40 minutes
PRAYER/CLOSING (pray together as a group, and then dismiss)	5 minutes	10 minutes

Group Dynamics

Leading a group through *Making Your Case for Christ* will prove to be highly rewarding both to you and your group members. However, this doesn't mean you will not encounter any challenges along the way. Discussions can get off track. Group members may not be sensitive to the needs and ideas of others. Some might worry they will be expected to talk about matters that make them feel awkward. Others may express comments that result in disagreements. To help ease any tensions, consider the following ground rules:

- When someone raises a question or comment that is off the main topic, suggest you deal with it another time. Or, if you feel led to go in that direction, let the group know you think it is an important question and will spend a few minutes discussing it.

- If someone asks a question you don't know how to answer, admit it and move on. If the matter seems important, tell them you'll look into it and bring back some thoughts about it the following week. Also, at your discretion, feel free to invite group members to comment on questions about which they might have some knowledge or insight.

- If you find one or two people are dominating the discussion time, direct a few questions to others in the group. Outside the main group time, ask the more dominating members to help you draw out the quieter ones. Work to make them a part of the solution instead of the problem.

- When a disagreement occurs, encourage group members to process the matter in love. Ask those on opposite sides to restate what they heard the other side say about it, and then invite each side to confirm whether or not that perception is accurate. Lead the group in examining Scripture or other relevant information in order to resolve the question. Or, if it's a peripheral issue assure them that it's sometimes best to simply agree to disagree (see Romans 14), and to move on to more important topics of discussion.

When any of these issues arise, encourage your group members to follow these biblical instructions: "Love one another" (John 13:34), "If it is possible, as far as it depends on you, live at peace with everyone" (Romans 12:18), and "Be quick to listen, slow to speak and slow to become angry" (James 1:19). This will help make your group time more positive and beneficial for everyone who attends.

Thank you again for your willingness to lead your group. May God bless your efforts and make your time together exceedingly fruitful and rewarding.

FOR FURTHER READING

BOOKS BY LEE STROBEL

The Case for Christ: A Journalist's Personal Investigation of the Evidence for Jesus (Grand Rapids, Mich.: Zondervan, 1998, updated and expanded edition, 2016).

The Case for Miracles: A Journalist Investigates Evidence for the Supernatural (Grand Rapids, Mich.: Zondervan, 2018).

The Case for Grace: A Journalist Explores the Evidence of Transformed Lives (Grand Rapids, Mich.: Zondervan, 2015).

In Defense of Jesus: Investigating Attacks on the Identity of Christ (Grand Rapids, Mich.: Zondervan, 2016; originally published as *The Case for the Real Jesus,* 2007).

The Case for a Creator: A Journalist Investigates Scientific Evidence That Points Toward God (Grand Rapids, Mich.: Zondervan, 2004).

The Case for Faith: A Journalist Investigates the Toughest Objections to Christianity (Grand Rapids, Mich.: Zondervan, 2000).

Note: Student and kids' editions of the above *Case* books are also available.

The Case for Hope: Looking Ahead with Confidence and Courage (Grand Rapids, Mich.: Zondervan, 2015).

The Case for Christianity Answer Book (Grand Rapids, Mich.: Zondervan, 2014).

The Case for Christ Study Bible: Investigating the Evidence for Belief (Grand Rapids, Mich.: Zondervan, 2010).

BOOKS BY LEE STROBEL AND MARK MITTELBERG

The Case for Christ Daily Moment of Truth (Grand Rapids, Mich.: Zondervan, 2018).

The Unexpected Adventure: Taking Everyday Risks to Talk with People about Jesus (Grand Rapids, Mich.: Zondervan, 2009).

BOOKS BY MARK MITTELBERG

Becoming a Contagious Christian (with Bill Hybels) (Grand Rapids, Mich.: Zondervan, 1994).

Becoming a Contagious Church: Increasing Your Church's Evangelistic Temperature (Grand Rapids, Mich.:Zondervan, 2007).

The Questions Christians Hope No One Will Ask (with Answers) (Carol Stream, Ill.: Tyndale, 2010).

The Reason Why: Faith Makes Sense (Carol Stream, Ill.: Tyndale, 2011).

Confident Faith: Building a Firm Foundation for Your Beliefs (Carol Stream, Ill.: Tyndale, 2013).

The Case for Christ Movie Edition

Solving the Biggest Mystery of All Time

Lee Strobel, *New York Times* Bestselling Author

Is there credible evidence that Jesus of Nazareth really is the Son of God?

Now a major motion picture, in *Case for Christ*, Strobel retraces his own spiritual journey from atheism and former legal editor of the *Chicago Tribune* to faith. Strobel cross-examines a dozen experts with doctorates from schools like Cambridge, Princeton, and Brandeis who are recognized authorities in their own fields. He challenges them with questions like, How reliable is the New Testament? Does evidence for Jesus exist outside the Bible? Is there any reason to believe the resurrection was an actual event?

Strobel's tough, point-blank questions read like a captivating, fast-paced novel. But it's not fiction. It's a riveting quest for the truth about history's most compelling figure.

The new edition includes scores of revisions and additions, including updated material on archaeological and manuscript discoveries, fresh recommendations for further study, and an interview with the author that tells dramatic stories about the book's impact, provides behind-the-scenes information, and responds to critiques of the book by skeptics. As *The Case for Christ* and its ancillary resources approach 10 million copies in print, this updated edition will prove even more valuable to contemporary readers.

The Unexpected Adventure

Taking Everyday Risks to Talk with People about Jesus

Lee Strobel and Mark Mittelberg, Bestselling Authors

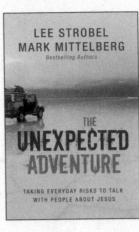

When we seize opportunities to talk with others about Jesus, days that start out dull and tedious can quickly blossom into exciting escapades.

Written for today's multigenerational, multicultural world, *The Unexpected Adventure* helps readers take easy steps into a natural evangelistic lifestyle that will energize their own faith while making an eternal difference in the lives of people they encounter.

Using a devotional-style format, bestselling authors Lee Strobel and Mark Mittelberg tell dramatic and sometimes funny stories from their own lives and then draw out practical applications backed by Scripture. Readers will be inspired with fresh compassion for their spiritually confused friends and equipped with practical strategies for influencing others for Christ. Entire churches will be rejuvenated as congregations discover that evangelism can be the adventure of a lifetime—starting today.

Available in stores and online!

The Case for Christ Video Study

Investigating the Evidence for Jesus

Lee Strobel and Garry Poole

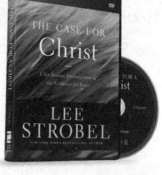

Is there credible evidence that Jesus of Nazareth really is the Son of God?

Skeptics dismiss the Jesus of the Gospels by claiming there is no evidence in the case for Christ. Lee Strobel disagrees. The former legal journalist and one-time atheist knows how to ask tough questions. His own search for truth about Jesus led him to faith in Christ.

Now Strobel invites you and your group to investigate the truth about Jesus Christ leading to the facts that guided Strobel from atheism to faith in Christ.

In this revised six-session study (DVD/digital video sold separately), participants will journey along with Strobel on a quest for the truth about Jesus. Rejecting easy answers, you will sift through fascinating historical evidence as you weigh compelling expert testimony.

In the end, groups may very well see Jesus in a new way—and even, like Strobel, find their life transformed.

Sessions include:

1. The Investigation of a Lifetime
2. Eyewitness Evidence
3. Evidence Outside the Bible
4. Analyzing Jesus
5. Evidence for the Resurrection
6. Reaching Your Verdict

Available in stores and online!

The Case for Christ Daily Moment of Truth

Lee Strobel and Mark Mittelberg

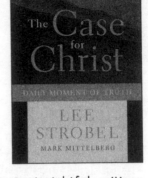

Why do we believe what we believe?

The Case for Christ Daily Moment of Truth, by leading apologists Lee Strobel and Mark Mittelberg, offers fact-based, intelligent devotions to build a foundational faith. These 180 insightful writings will strengthen your spiritual knowledge and touch your heart with life-changing truth.

Topics range from scientific discoveries to theological explanations, and each devotion is followed by a brief reflection, prayer, and thought to meditate on and talk about.

You'll emerge with a deeper understanding of your beliefs. In the process, you'll find your love of truth—and your passion to share it—growing each day.

Available in stores and online!

The Case for Miracles

A Journalist Investigates Evidence for the Supernatural

Lee Strobel, *New York Times* Bestselling Author

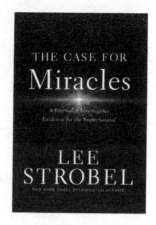

New York Times bestselling author Lee Strobel trains his investigative sights on the hot-button issue of whether it's credible to believe God intervenes supernaturally in people's lives today.

This provocative book starts with an unlikely interview in which America's foremost skeptic builds a seemingly persuasive case *against* the miraculous. But then Strobel travels the country to quiz scholars to see whether they can offer solid answers to atheist objections. Along the way, he encounters astounding accounts of healings and other phenomena that simply cannot be explained away by naturalistic causes. The book features the results of exclusive new scientific polling that shows miracle accounts are much more common than people think.

What's more, Strobel delves into the most controversial question of all: what about miracles that *don't* happen? If God *can* intervene in the world, why doesn't he do it more often to relieve suffering? Many American Christians are embarrassed by the supernatural, not wanting to look odd or extreme to their neighbors. Yet, *The Case for Miracles* shows not only that the miraculous is possible but that God still does intervene in our world in awe-inspiring ways. Here's a unique book that examines all sides of this issue and comes away with a passionate defense for God's divine action in lives today.

Available in stores and online!